On the Days I Act Up

Kelly Stewart

2007

ISBN: 978-1-4357-0187-8

Introduction:

This book is dedicated to the many people that I have met over the years, which I have been fortunate enough to call my friends.

Their ability to story tell, share a moment with others, and to be able to make people feel good about themselves, make them all very unique individuals.

Unfortunately, a lot of them have left us and moved on to another place in this life, leaving a few of us behind to tell the tales that they passed on when here on earth.

So now I pass on these tales so that when someone asks Grandma what Grandpa was like, she can curl up in a chair, and share the same story that brings a smile to my face every time I remember it.

And that will bring peace and happiness to me, as I know there will be "one hell of a tale being told" around the gates of heaven, once all of these characters are reunited!

This story is for you my good friends.

Working for a Living

Over the years I have found out that working takes up a great deal of a person's life. Almost to the point where you are at work more than you are at home. Therefore it only makes sense that if you work in a place for a long enough time, your co-workers actually become like family. To the point that you fight with them, complain about them, and when they are gone from your life on a daily basis, you actually start to miss them.

Thank God I only worked in one place for a really long time!

Actually I am like a politician with dyslexia. I started out working for the Federal Government, went to the Provincial Government, and finally ended up working for Municipal Government. Usually in this day in age, you see people trying to go the other way.

I was lucky enough to hold other jobs before becoming the evil "civil servant" that most people refer to. Usually brought to light around election time but not usually mentioned when picking up an unemployment check, baby bonus, health card, social services or some of the other many things.

Like I said, I was very fortunate to start my journey outside the world of the government, which gave me a unique perspective to all sides of the story. In keeping with the idea that this book is built on humor, I will not get into the pros and cons that we all discuss, especially after a few drinks. I see now why they used to shut down the local watering holes on election days. Some people should be banned from alcohol for the whole campaign possibly.

My take will involve some of the more unique things I noticed along the way but I will point out that this span compiles over twenty years in three different tiers of government. I have seen too many staff, not enough staff, and more work for a few staff left. So bear with me and try to figure out the years that my story happened and when I mention a leaders name, stay focused on the story, don't get sidetracked by some old memories, either good or bad.

I think one of my first jobs was delivering the Toronto Star as a boy. I remember the tips at Christmas, the extra spending money, and most of all, the Christmas edition. One year the paper had three hundred and sixty-five pages, which meant that I could only get four papers in my bag at a time. That built character, and also explains why my knuckles used to drag on the ground when I walked. It only straightened out once I got my beer belly, which forced my arms upward and outward.

From there I progressed to working on the local garbage truck every Saturday morning. I think I was around fourteen at the time. The garbage truck was an old Brewer's Retail truck, which of course had no compacter. The compacter came from two of us stomping garbage down in the truck to try and avoid an extra trip to the dump and back to unload.

The garbage truck continued to build character and reaffirms my belief that a person can find work if they are willing. I find the problem with some kids today is that they expect to start at the top, or to have something given to them. It used to be a boot in the ass, but maybe in today's day and age, they are the ones that are right, and I am just getting old.

Now normally Donnie and I would work on the truck with his Dad, which was good. The bad part would be when his Dad got called into his regular job for overtime on Saturday. That meant that Donnie would drive and I would recruit a friend, or Donnie would bring somebody to help.

There was one major difference when Donnie drove. On the regular days when his dad was there, his dad would get out and help at the big stops like the grocery store, but when Donnie drove, he would lock himself in and sleep.

This of course led to the first rebellion ever in garbage truck history in the Village of Marmora.

The first problem that arose was that the truck was a standard. The second was that I was only fourteen, as was my helper that day, but for some reason we didn't care. After two stops with him sleeping, we plotted our plan of attack.

At one of the regular stops along the way, we requested his help to lift something heavy. When he came to the back, I grabbed him and the other lad jumped into the front of the truck. The rest of the trip down the street consisted of him grumbling while loading garbage into the truck, which was overshadowed by the sound of grinding gears while my accomplice tried to figure out how to drive a standard.

The only other time we rebelled involved finding a whole bunch of turnips that someone had thrown out. When he wouldn't leave the heated cab, we decided it was time to bombard him with vegetables until he got out. It wasn't long before he gave in and started helping us again, but the mess and the look of the truck ended up getting the whole trio in trouble when we got back to the yard.

I finished high school at seventeen in January. It was after the semester system had come in, which meant that a person could finish their grade twelve half way through the school year. That could have been a good thing or a bad thing depending on what you planned to do for that extra half of a year.

Being the smart man I was; it gave me the opportunity to work full time and save some money before going to college in the fall. I thought possibly something in Science or Business, because they had been my strengths in high school.

I don't know if it was my first full week paycheck, buying my first truck, or just having a lot of spending money in the bank, that made me sway from my original plan. I was still living at home and a full time job was a nice thing with hardly any expenses. That would change as I found out later in life.

Paying for a vehicle while living with your parents is easy. Getting up for work on a daily basis after the novelty wears off, is not.

I started work at a cheese factory while I was still in high school. I worked on the weekends and during the summer. Working there taught me two very important lessons. One being what it was like to do a hard day's work, and the other, what it was like to drink afterwards.

Anyone that knows me now, will find this hard to believe. I didn't really drink very much until my good friends at the cheese factory taught me how.

And what a fine job they did of that! They used to collect money from everyone that could stay after work, the key words being "able to stay". It used to be two dollars, each which would usually haul a twenty-four and a twelve each night. One person would volunteer to collect and drive downtown to get the beer while the others cleaned up.

The other thing I learned besides "how to drink" was "how to volunteer". Cleanup or get the beer; wasn't really something I had to decide too long on to make a decision.

At first I was reluctant to stay for beer because I had my Dad's car, but by the time I ended up leaving the cheese factory, I was the one organizing the wind down party afterwards.

One of the most memorable occasions was the planning of a get together, just prior to Christmas, where I had everyone put in five dollars instead of two. How proud I was returning to the plant with three twenty-fours and a twelve of beer.

The problem was it was right before Christmas. The regulars all had to go home and only had two beer each leaving us well over two twenty-fours to split up and take. Some of them didn't even want to do that.

What made the night memorable was my co-worker who was also my best man when I got married, chose Ford trucks ahead of anything else. This particular truck had a problem with the kingpins, tie rods, steering arms, or whatever to hell makes the thing drive straight while travelling down the road.

I did not like driving his truck when sober because it travelled back and forth across the road like you have just run over a family of porcupines, (and no porcupines were hurt during this adventure).

I did notice that the truck drove much better, after a few drinks, but that could be because it was built back in the days when "drinking and driving was legal". Do you remember that time?

I guess there wasn't really such a time, but back then I was too young and foolish to realize how much money a man could spend on insurance in the next fifteen years.

Getting back to the story, we had packed all the beer we could behind the seat of my friend's truck and headed out for home. Apparently we decided to use some type of sign language to communicate along with our slurred English on our voyage. I know that now because the police officer said that one of the reasons he stopped us was because of the puppet show he witnessed through the back window. The other would have been the vehicle movement.

Anyone that drinks knows that you sometimes need to use your hands to relay a point to someone. That day it might have been excessive, somewhat to the point that all four hands were moving and none were left in the ten and two position on the steering wheel.

We had travelled over thirty miles and were only a quarter mile from home when we were stopped. It started with the, "Hello sir, have you been drinking?" It ended with "your friend has had too much to drink and you will have to drive."

This is the part to remember where a) the way the truck drives on a good day and b) I was the organizer of the Christmas bash because c) I didn't have to drive! All valid points like the "drinking and driving being legal that year". I thought for some reason that it wasn't the proper time to bring it up.

As the police officer came back to the truck and my friend climbed into the passenger side, I slipped into the driver's seat. With a panic ridden face I attempted to start the truck without worrying about how the damn thing was going to steer while going down the road. I couldn't even have a beer because the police officer took them all with him.

I was starting to panic when I couldn't get the truck started when I heard a tap on the window. The nice officer then handed me the keys to the truck through the window. The next quarter mile was the longest I have ever driven in my life while awake!

Another story that comes to mind while there involved two shifts. There was the early morning shift and the day shift. The problem with the day shift was that a lot of times you had to pass through the lunchroom, just when the early morning shift, were having their lunch.

This particular time involved the morning shift picking up lunch from A & W. All I could smell was a Poppa Burger with my name on it. After all there were two on the table, and I left one of my sandwiches as a trade for the second one.

I found out at this time, there are two sacred things in the cheese business, one being a man's hot lunch and the other his locker. The result was being chased through the plant until I was cornered and had a pickaxe put through my hard hat with a warning that next time my head would be in it. The second was my locker being glued shut with my street clothes still in it. The third was my boss staring at me while I was trying to use a crow bar to get into my brand new locker. All three were not good!

Earlier I made mention of having beer after work for those that could stay. Apparently that doesn't apply if you are new or are young. It actually would get to the point that someone would take your car keys and wouldn't give them back unless you stayed for beer.

Two interesting facts about this ritual were if you were smart enough to keep your keys on you while working, they would block you in with four other vehicles. The other would be to try and get to your vehicle so that you had to stay.

The shocker of all days was when I saw my dad's car "76 Dodge Monaco" going by the building when I knew I had the keys in my pocket. I thought to my self that the crazy bastards had made a duplicate set of keys from the ones in my locker. That act in itself would almost be criminal!

When I came out, my mentor and friend who we called "Homer", had used the keys from his "67 Chrysler named Black Bart" to start my dads car. I didn't believe him at first, but after trying my keys in his car, around the building I drove.

Learning from him was a good way for any young lad to start out. Work hard and play hard, but remember the work is always there the next day. They would give you one day with a hangover but if you didn't dig in your heels and pull your weight the next day, you would definitely hear about it. That was another lesson that stuck with me throughout life.

Another important lesson was when I first received my Fourth Class Stationary Engineering, which I achieved through correspondence courses from the University of Southern Alberta and the trades program in Ontario. I was flying around the room thinking I had achieved so much and that now "I was that much smarter than I was before". After watching me for a while he pointed out that "he had more knowledge in his thumb than what that license gave me". Like any young lad, I was ticked to the nines, a little hurt, a little disappointed, and very frustrated.

Then after some time, and some thought, it became clear what he was trying to do. He wanted to give me the foresight to see what the world ahead would bring, and not to get too far ahead of yourself, or forget where you are and where you began. That had to be the best advice anyone has ever given me.

Now on a less serious note, I also learned the phrase, "Too old a cat to be screwed by a kitten."

Homer and his son and daughter-in-law were involved in the horse racing business. I myself started when I was around seven, riding in the back of the horse trailer with my cousin Johnny and good old "Single Elgin". He would turn out to be the horse that would likely be responsible for my "gambling addiction". That and possibly some genes that came from a long line of people that would bet on anything from when the "Mayflower was going to land" to "if break open tickets were invented yet".

If they had of been, I would have liked to seen the hull of the ship when it landed. It would be the only ship in the history books with a sail made out of "cherries, lemons, bells and bars".

On this particular occasion, we were gathered at the Stirling Fair Grounds where they kept their racehorse "Moonlight Peggy", and another little pony that I can't remember its name. The reason I don't bother to remember it or care if I ever hear about it anymore is due to what we ended up doing together that eventful day.

Somewhere between having a social drink while working the racehorse and my friend's daughter riding her pony, a very strange opportunity for me to make some "easy money" happened. It seemed "Homer" who was into his fifties by now, developed a very weak moment and bet me that he could beat me once around the track with a ten speed, before I could get there with the pony.

It should have been like "taking candy from a baby"? Of course I was a little skeptical having dealt with this bunch on other side bets from before, but being the smart man that I am, I sent my friend's daughter around the track once to see if the pony knew the route. Sure enough it did it like clockwork, and I placed the wager with strict confidence.

I should have known by the sheepish smile on my friend's face, another person from our wedding party. It was his dad that I was racing, but solidarity should have prevailed between us and he should have informed me of any inside information. Or so I thought!

When the race began, the pony and I took off and had a half of the oval covered before Homer got on the bike. The only sound I could make out was the noise of Homer laughing and coughing as he started towards me, still a quarter of the track away. I thought I would make it sporting and actually wait until he closed the distance a little closer, before trotting on in for the victory.

The closer he came to me, the louder the laughter and the coughing, almost to the point where I thought he was going to fall of the bike. I decided it was time to make my final move to the finish.

The pony decided it was time to eat! I don't mean have a quick bite and get back in the race, but more like "Sorry I am on lunch, try again in a half hour".

Homer went by and the pony didn't care. I actually think he might have nodded at him on the way by. I tried kicking, nudging, asking, yelling, pulling and finally standing beside the pony as Homer crossed the finish line, much to the amusement of his family. Especially his granddaughter, who couldn't quit giggling even as she came out and got the pony to ride the rest of the way to the finish.

It was on that day, that I learned "I was too young a kitten to screw a cat".

Those old times at the fairgrounds were memorable, reinforcing something that we all tend to forget anymore. It is possible to make your own fun, and share a laugh between friends, without the big expense of what we expect today.

In my very first full time job, I was very lucky to work for a well respected developed company who had the knack to hire family oriented people to run their day to day operations.

Those people taught me the importance of hard work, family, dedication and commitment to making any business work.

Something I will never forget!

To recap things a bit, remember I was supposed to be in my first full time job from January until the following September, in which I was leaving for College. Well something went off schedule along the way.

My career path changed from going to college to becoming a Cheese Maker, and then a Butter Maker once I started to receive those weekly checks.

The Cheese Maker thing was a good idea, except there was also a room full of people thinking the same idea, so I couldn't really see that happen. The Butter Maker thing was promising until they found out I couldn't stand the taste of butter, which happened to be a very important part of that process.

Being a laborer wasn't such a bad thing but it was going to limit my income and the ability to progress in the future.

I was quite content until I noticed a summer student from Queens looking at the 4th Class Stationary Engineering books. Once I took a look at them I was hooked, and thus started down a new branch in my road that I was about to travel. One that I had never prepared for in High School but would get me to where I am today.

My only regret is that my father had taught me that they were two distinct routes, University or College, and the Trades. At the time that was the common way of thinking, but became evidently clear later in history that as a culture we weren't living up to our potential.

When I first started in the business, I had a tool chest full of tools and everything was mechanical. I now have the same tool chest with a laptop computer, which can make changes at any remote location instantaneously.

The change in how things are done was something that both sides of the fence had to learn after leaving high school. I think in today's day and age that thinking has left and we will see the future start to provide the whole picture instead of just pieces.

A chance came for me to progress in my Stationary Engineering with a different company, and with some regret I had to make the decision to leave my friends and head out on a new adventure.

It was in the wood manufacturing business, which off course boils down to production numbers. I worked steady afternoons looking after the steam boilers, heating and maintenance, which lead to a lead hand position.

Now a lead hand position isn't really anymore than being able to wear the hall monitor's sash in little school. You can think you are important, you can act important, and you can "tell on people". Either way you will still end up upside down in a garbage can before the shift is out.

I decided to use it as a building tool instead of something of importance, which worked great with the rest of the people on the afternoon shift. Instead of intimidating them, I was there to help. The whole process would lead to eventually a foreman's job but as I was progressing with my Stationary Engineering, I was ready to move on to a bigger plant after a just a couple of years.

The move took me to a major food processing plant, which involved mostly one thing, "Ammonia". Now a basic rule for anyone to follow is if you trap steam between two points, it will eventually cool and condense back to water. Ammonia on the other hand, boils below room temperature, and will continue to build pressure until something finally explodes.

It was a state of the art plant, a world known company, very good money, but unfortunately, and "twenty thousand pounds of ammonia".

If I hadn't mentioned it earlier, ammonia also has the ability to scavenge oxygen from anywhere it can get it, mainly the "stuff you are trying to breathe". It also goes to anywhere there is moisture on your body and burns, so try to figure that out while holding your armpits, balls and asshole, while trying to get your breath back!

If you haven't noticed yet, I was a little intimidated so I was actually surprised that I made it six months.

While there I did have a couple of events worth mentioning. The first one involved a thing called a "Steam Generator". The best way to describe it to you is like a big still, in which water enters the bottom through a big coil. The coil is heated and as the water travels through it, steam comes out the top. It is so simple that your kid's should be able to run it.

The lesson to learn out of this is to try and not be doing something else when you are starting this up. See it involves starting the unit up, with the discharge valve closed. A lot like boiling your kettle and putting duct tape over the hole where the steam comes out. You can get away with it at the start but you better let that pressure go somewhere, or it will go off worse than your mother-in-law when you are late for Christmas dinner.

The other thing to remember is that there are miles and miles of pipeline that did have steam in them at one time. We have already learned that steam turns to water when we leave it alone for a while. So therefore it is very important to introduce the steam to these lines in a very gentle manner, so as to push the water out of the lines in a nice controlled fashion.

Much the same as pulling the duct tape off the kettle in a slow motion and not all at once.

The people that design these systems know the problem and cleverly place traps above the ceiling tiles throughout the plant that collect the water from the pipes as it is pushed out of the system at start up. They are very smart people that help operators like us everyday.

I think I did say to try and not be doing anything else when this process is taking place. On this particular day, I think I was.

Old Jenny, as I referred to her, was starting to puff and puff, and was doing what she normally did, when I decided I had time to finish one last lab test. I then noticed her pressure starting to rise as I started to climb up onto to her to open the discharge valve.

Somewhere along the way I lost my footing and came crashing to the floor while Jenny started to make noises like a girl on frosh night after a keg of whiskey. She started making these deep bellowing sounds while shaking like she was having a convulsion. Her pressure was continuing to rise and she looked like she was going to blow a safety valve.

Finally I regained my footing and climbed back on her, climbing for her release valve. But instead of releasing it slowly, I panicked like a high school kid on prom night, and let it go all at once. The rest made history!

Picture the look on a room full of men and women at four in the morning, with their hairnets wet, the ceiling tiles dripping down on them, and this constant look of confusion. Them all looking at me in which I could only reply, "There was this valve that failed, shouldn't happen again."

I ended up only working six months at this place, but in the short time I was there I was left with a couple of stories that just have to be passed on.

The first involved the rules of the company. Seeing it was a food processing plant there were mainly two rules that applied above all. They were no drinking on the job, and secondly, under no circumstances were you able to eat the food they were making.

At that point in my life, both seemed very fair. I had enough food to keep me happy during a normal shift and secondly, I liked going to work to get a break from the drinking. Sort of like taking a holiday and recounting what the weekend was like, if you know what I mean.

I thought that some staff was probably breaking the first rule on the first day I worked a weekend shift. While making my rounds as a makeshift security person along with my regular duties, I happened to notice a set of legs coming out of one of the product bins. It looked a lot like an old tomcat scrounging for food in a dumpster.

When I got closer to the bin, I just stared at the person in amazement, until I got their reply, "Who to hell are you?" they said. Once I filled them in on whom I was; I mentioned the thing about not eating any of the products. Their response was they were getting lunch and asked me if I wanted any. I thought at that time how foolish it would be to lose your job over a microwavable dinner and promised myself that I would never do that under any circumstances.

Then unfortunately one night it happened. I somehow had eaten my whole lunch bag full of food in the first half hour that I was on the midnight shift. That was not a problem until four in the morning when I could smell Salisbury steak cooking in the other room. I did my best to try and forget the smell but damn it was good.

After much thought and discussion with myself, I decided to head out to the production room where the smell became even more overwhelmingly.

I had to devise some type of plan, a distraction of some type to get the sweet smelling meat without being noticed.

When I got to the end of the extremely large cook oven, I noticed someone who looked a lot like a defenseman on our hockey team. I no longer needed a plan but just needed to ask.

While I pleaded my case on hunger and starvation, I was told to "just take it and go on", which I gladly did.

If you happen to be like me then you will know that anytime, and I mean anytime, you try to do something shady, or against the rules, someone or something will intervene. This case was the same.

With my almost too hot to handle Salisbury steak in hand, I proceeded back to the confines of the operations office, far away from the production area. My thoughts were that once there I could sit down and enjoy this beautiful piece of steak, which was so overwhelmingly delicious smelling. It was not to be!

Over the years our hockey team had been holding slow pitch tournaments on a regular basis each year. Suddenly and without warning, the production supervisor, who played for one of the regular teams that attended the tournament each year, decided to come and visit me.

If you have an illegal Salisbury steak in one hand, and a supervisor coming to visit on the other hand, than "Houston, we do have a problem!"

The average person would likely not have let it bother them, and then likely made some excuse to leave. I on the other hand decided to try and hide the steak in the left hand pocket of my coveralls. It seemed like a good idea until I remembered the steak was still quite hot for the hands to hold onto.

The next five minutes involved a lot of jibber jabber small talk, while the nipple closest to my heart was starting to burn off. Throughout the conversation I endured the pain, knowing that I would have my Salisbury steak when this person finally left me alone. That moment finally arrived.

As I rushed outside to let out a yelp of pain, I pulled the beautiful steak from its pouch, only to find it covered in sawdust and dirt. All was for nothing until I heard a noise from the dumpster next to me. There standing looking at me, was the scruffiest, homeliest, beat up tomcat, a man had ever seen. The dark saddened eyes and the long drawn out, "MEOOOOW".

I replied that, "Today is your lucky day", as I threw him my sawdust, dirt covered steak.

What started out looking like someone scrounging through a dumpster for food, actually ended up feeding something doing the same? A little ironic isn't it?

The most memorable and enlightened tale that I can recount was that of a man that I had the privilege to work with at this company. He was such a kind and determined man. The type of man that most could not understand, unless you too saw life through his eyes, and felt the feelings that he felt, as he travelled along life's journey.

We actually only had the chance to share one amazing story on a Sunday morning when he was finishing his midnight shift. He asked me if I wanted a coffee, before he left, while he told me a tale.

As he poured the coffee into my cup, it told me a lot about the man, his travels, his triumphs and tribulations. As I took a sip out of the coffee he had poured me, it suddenly told me more.

I tried to contact him a few years later after I had left the company to find only his widow, who informed me of his passing. A shame because the world lost one of the best storytellers and one of the best men it had ever produced on that sad, dark day. Humanity lost not only a soul, but also an icon, and I learned this all in one brief visit with him. This is his story.

Year's back there was construction going on at the south bridge on Highway #2 in the city of Trenton, Ontario. Trenton being home to one of the largest, if not the largest air bases in Canada.

While construction was under way, it proved the congestion of the traffic at the bridge in the afternoon was too much for the temporary set of traffic lights. They decided that they needed police to do traffic control to help through rush hour. Now that you know that part, our story can begin.

It seemed that my friend had the weekend off and was invited to his brother's in Bancroft. He told me that the best way to get twelve cans of beer cold was to put them in front of the grill of you car and as you drove, the cold air was drawn in over them. I always wondered that if you had a twenty-four, your car would likely overheat.

Anyhow, he headed to Bancroft with twelve cans of beer under the hood and a sixty-six-ounce bottle of rye under his seat.

When he arrived, his brother greeted him, but when he went to take out his booze, his brother informed him that he would be extremely offended if he tried to bring it inside. His brother said that he was the host and they were going to drink his supply.

None of that seemed to be a problem until three weeks later. When my friend came home, he remembered to take out the beer from the front of the car, but forgot about the bottle under the seat. That itself wouldn't be a problem until later in the week.

On the last shift of the week my friend was returning home looking for a relaxing long weekend. Of course until he got to the bridge in Trenton, where he wasn't really paying attention until the car in front of him came to a sudden, abrupt stop.

With that, the bottle of whiskey under the seat decided to shoot up under his feet. Normally not a problem until you realize that a traffic cop is only about thirty yards away signaling you to stop with the normal hand outward motion.

Still not normally a problem, until you decide to readjust the bottle back under the seat, which happens to lead to the following. First the base of the bottle shoots under the brake pedal while the neck of the bottle gets stuck over the gas pedal, which is not a good scene!

Picture the next set of events as they unfold.

There at the corner was a police officer giving the stop command using the well-known hand signal.

My friend who was trying to push down on the brake, which in turn, revs the engine, and makes the car jump towards the police officer.

Which is followed, by an even more very angry police officer, who is reissuing the stop command, again?

My friend with both feet on the break peddle, the car revving, and jumping towards the already pissed off police officer.

The finally "I have had enough with this asshole" pissed off police officer heading directly towards you until luck intervenes.

Some lady drives right through the stoplight and into someone else and the police officer gives you the "go right now" signal.

The whiskey bottle, finally let's lose and you get it back under the seat.

I retell a true classic tale that actually happened to my very good friend.

May the angels look after you my friend?

Backing up the story line a little, I had worked hard, written and received my next level of license, being my 3rd Class Stationary Engineering. I had finished it while working afternoons in the wood processing plant, which enabled me to take the next job along the way, at the food processing plant.

This is where one of "Homer's" lessons came into play, being "don't get too far ahead of your self."

I had progressed very well and fast with the written bookwork, but found myself lacking in the "on the job" skills that can only be acquired by experience. This became most evident with my inexperience with ammonia and refrigeration at the food processing plant to the point it became very uncomfortable.

As I crested the six month mark, I found myself surrounded with great people and a beautiful plant, but afraid of some of the situations which might happen when on a shift by my self. Thunderstorms there could be disastrous!

I decided that it was time to make a move elsewhere, when one day fate took a strange twist, and I received a phone call while home on my day off. It was from the wood processing plant and while on the phone they offered me the afternoon foreman's job.

It was strange timing, but a very welcome call to return to something I felt comfortable doing. The only downfall was back to steady afternoons.

Originally when I had started at the wood processing plant on the afternoon shift, I was greeted by what I thought was one of the most grumpy, hard nosed people I had ever met. I would find out over the next two years that he was actually a kind, caring individual, whose only downfall, was trying to work while putting up with the pain he had.

When I had left the first time, his pain was getting worse, and there was some hint at that time of a foreman's job, but I said that I would only be interested when he said that he was done. I wished in a way that things had worked out so that I could have spent the last six months with him before he retired.

He is another friend that has left this world for another place, but before going, he left me with some great memories, which I will share with you.

On afternoon shift, we didn't take on a lot of maintenance, except for breakdowns, and the odd minor repair. Instead that type of work was left for the millwrights on day shifts, which obviously were better trained.

For whatever particular reason, the boss thought that I should learn how to weld one night. I had welded a little before but only on two different pieces of metal laying flat on the ground. This on the other had involved welding on a piece that was upright, which can be quite a challenge!

During this welding process, I felt this burning sensation on my beer belly and looked down to see I was burning tiny holes in the front of my shirt. After some searching I located an old pair of coveralls, which I slid my arms through and wore backwards to protect myself from the sparks.

All in all it seemed like a good idea at the time, but I couldn't believe how much smoke there was from just a little bit of welding. That was until I noticed the legs of the coveralls were on fire!

I quickly did my rendition of the "Tetley Tea Folk, Folk Dance" to get the situation under control. As I stomped out the flames, I decided it was a prudent time to finish this little exercise before something bigger happened.

So as I put the finishing touches on the piece, I then removed my coveralls and took them out back to the wooden board where they had been hanging previously. Finally I was done.

The boss came along and inspected the work. He suggested I grind it down and paint it while he went back to the office to do paperwork. It wasn't really that big of a job and turned out to be even more relaxing once I started painting.

The only part I found really confusing was how much smoke was still in the air since I had quit welding. It even seemed to be getting worse, if that made any sense? It was almost getting irritating at one point, almost to the point where it looked like the smoke was coming from the other room, so I went to investigate.

When I went in the other room I found the coveralls were missing. Well not actually just one pair, but three pairs and a rain coat that all had been hanging next to the electrical box on the wooden board. What I found instead was burning embers of plywood, something frowned upon when you have a whole building full of wood and sawdust.

Once the original panic attack was over, I grabbed a fire extinguisher and put out the blaze. What I was left with was a charbroiled chunk of wood adjacent to one of the main electrical panels that someone had to volunteer to tell the boss about. Unfortunately, that person turned out to be me.

What I was expecting was a lashing, a lecture and a reprimand. What I received was a look, a chuckle and "You better make that look better before the dayshift comes in". The look on my face was like taking your dog to the vet and watching them remove quills while your dog sits there quiet.

The rest of the night involved a lot of scraping and a couple coats of paint but seeing I was actually working under the day shift Maintenance Foreman, I wasn't quite out of the woods yet. The next afternoon would tell the tale.

Of course I had pretty well forgotten about the incident until I arrived at the plant the next afternoon. I was greeted by the maintenance Foreman who told me to follow him out to the boiler room. He asked me, "Do you want to explain? I replied, "I was learning how to weld, so I could help out the dayshift." He told me that in the future, they would be ok on their own, and to stay away from the welder, which didn't really hurt my feelings at that point.

He also told me that I could explain to the men where their coveralls were. Apparently Millwrights will wash their coveralls in paint thinner to get rid of the grease. I found out that paint thinner, plus cloth, plus sparks, equals a lot of tension and explaining. Something I think you should stay away from in the future.

The other story involves meeting the wife of my boss at Christmas time. She was an extremely pleasant woman with a great sense of humor and as we talked, it became evident on how family oriented they were. That has always been a big trait of mine, and something that I am very proud of.

It turned out that they would board kids each summer when they came to work for Ontario Hydro. It also became evident that they would become very close with the kids before the summer was out, which led to a lot of mischievous pranks between the two parties.

It would involve shorted sheets, mismatched socks; just about anything was fair game. The classic of all came in the summer that

I had met them, in which it was a ritual for his wife and their border to work nightly on an enormous jig saw puzzle. The kids were a long way from home and staying with a family like your own was very important to being away.

Throughout the summer they worked together on this puzzle, which covered the whole dining room table. It became more and more frustrating in the final days before the young lad returned home, because they were so close to finishing it, but was missing three pieces. They looked high and low, searching the whole house for the missing pieces but were unable to finish before they said their goodbyes.

After the young lad had left, she continued to search for those three pieces, becoming more and more frustrated at where they had gone, until she finally gave up.

Christmas time arrived and with it came a card from their young border wishing them well in the holiday season and thanking them for their kindness over the summer.

The last line of the card read something like this, "And by the way, I thought maybe you could use these."

As she read the card she turned the envelope upside down and watched the three pieces of the puzzle fall out onto the table.

"Damn him" were the words, as a smile came over her face, and as a tear came to her eye. That was a summer that would never be forgotten by either one.

Returning to the wood processing plant as foreman was quite an easy transition, because everyone knew me and we had already worked together for a couple of years. It gave me some insight into what it takes to make a place survive, which basically boils down to the numbers produced versus the waste produced. We needed to hit a 70% production target to be profitable, and with the raw material being provided, those numbers were sometimes hard or impossible to achieve.

I took flack from the Superintendent one day for letting my shift leave earlier by three minutes before the end of the two a.m. quitting time. My thought was that the people work hard and they are on steady afternoons, so giving them a small break wasn't that big a problem.

His reply was three minutes' times twenty people equals an hour of lost production. A very good insight if you are in a boardroom full of people and trying to make the math work when finding ways to increase production. Mine was a lot simpler than that.

Maybe treat the people like people, and they will go the extra mile when you ask them to. In my year at the plant as foreman, that was never a problem.

Now that I think back, a couple of things come to mind, when I was working as foreman. I carried a more serious role of course, which led to less time to get sidetracked thinking up the weird and wonderful things that I do. There was one in particular that I remembered that lead back to when I was working as a lead hand just prior to leaving. It involved Barb.

I apparently said one night to Barb, who I thought wasn't pulling her weight that if I ever become foreman than the first thing I was going to do was to fire her. She apparently had ticked me off at something that night, and I eventually lost my cool.

The one thing to remember is that I don't usually keep a journal of people "to be fired if I ever become foreman list". The other thing to remember is that Barb apparently keeps a journal of the people "that will likely fire me if they become foreman list."

I had apparently forgotten about it but she apparently had not. So much so, that it lead to her crying in the bathroom and the then lead hand coming to tell me that I should talk with Barb. Once I had been filled in to what this was all about, I quickly went to find Barb and straightened out the misconception. I ensured her that I couldn't fire her tonight because I didn't have a replacement handy, so she was likely safe until tomorrow. Then I told her I was kidding! My suggestion is to maybe watch what you say because there may be actually someone that takes you seriously. Go figure?

Also while working there I met a husband and wife that had immigrated to Canada years earlier. Over the years as the company had changed names and owners, these two individuals had been there from pretty well day one.

I used to enjoy listening to some of their stories they told because the wife was more fluent in English, and the husband had possibly about a hundred words or so that he used. So like most married couples, the wife did all the talking and he used to just nod quite a bit. When we were alone we would share some tales and it turned out that we both had something in common. That turned out to be that we both thought that "drinking" was a good way to pass the day when you were off.

His wife told me a story of how she couldn't believe how her husband would get so tired while doing the chores at home on the weekend. He would go out in the morning on their farm, come in at lunch, have one drink and return back out to farming in the afternoon. By nighttime he would come in and have supper but then want to lie down and go to sleep.

That was until the day she followed him around on his chores without him seeing her. She apparently found "Mickey bottles" on the tractor, in the barn, in the drive shed, and a couple of more isolated spots. His secret to farming happily on the weekend was out. That is why I hide my bottles in my wife's stuff because she never thinks to check there.

One of the most different nights there involved the night watchman calling in sick, and me having to stay and watch the place until morning until I could find a replacement.

You see there was a bit of an unwritten rule that stated if we could get all the product processed before the end of the shift, we would quit early and the whole bunch of us would head to the hotel on any Friday night for last call.

Two of the leaders of the pack were girls who would start yelling out the words "cattle call" as they could see the production schedule winding down. I call them girls but both were women so they should have been at an age where they weren't quite as devilish as they were when they were younger. I was definitely wrong.

After informing them that I would not be participating in the "cattle call" this evening due to the night watchman duties, I bid them a goodnight. I thought that would be the end of it, until at two in the morning I see a car outside. I went to the door and met the two of them carrying what looked like a four foot by four foot "STOP" sign, which they thought I should keep for them because the town police officer was after them.

A quick recall of the evening provided what I thought was true. First I said that I would not be participating in the "cattle call" frenzy this evening. Second I was working and last but not least, I wouldn't have stolen a "STOP" sign. Not even the regular one-foot, by one foot one, let alone a four by four foot one.

I am also pretty well positive that I wouldn't take it back to my workplace to have my foreman hold it for me until things cooled off. I suggested that maybe they should return it to where they had taken it, but they said they couldn't because they were scared. Can you imagine?

Well they headed off on their merry but very disturbed way, and it wasn't long before the local police showed up. He for some reason thought that maybe I should know where the missing "STOP" sign had gone, and at one point thought I was involved.

After seeing that I was working and that I could possibly get a hold of the culprits responsible, he left me with the following advice, "Tell those girls to have that sign back in place before I get my paperwork done in an hour!"

After he left, I made the call and passed on the message. When I went home in the morning I see that the sign had been returned to its proper place and that there were no sign around town of the two girls that were obviously destined for the doghouse!

That had to be one of the most interesting nights while working there.

After about a year as foreman and my name being thrown into the ring as Plant Manager for a different division, I was quite excited to take on this new opportunity. I prepared thoroughly and attended the interview process, which involved only one other person who had no knowledge of the wood manufacturing process, so I felt my chance was very good.

That was until the announcement came out that the new Plant Manager was no other than the husband of the daughter of the owner. From there everything sort of went south, so I continued on in my afternoon shift and watched as the new Manager of the other division fall deeper and deeper into problems which eventually led to selling off everything the family owned. I decided to get out just prior to that.

I found out that if you leave one job, it is a good idea to have another or before you know it the bills will start to build up. I was fortunate to be able to go and work for my wife's uncle who was in the tree business at the time. It was very hard work but was also likely the last time I was ever in shape since leaving the cheese factory.

About that time, I had a chance for an interview with Bell Canada. The only draw back was they were hiring part time help consisting of forty hours per week for only possibly a three-year stint, without any guarantee. Still it was the first time Bell had hired in years, so it sounded like a great opportunity.

This is where the second strange occurrence with fate happened. I just got finished hanging up the phone after talking with the person that was going to be doing the interviewing for Bell Telephone with the last name Cook. Just after the phone was hung up, it rang again and the man on the phone introduced himself as so and so Cook. I asked him did we just not speak, and he replied no that we had not, but he knew I was out of work and that I had a 3rd Class Stationary Engineers license and asked if I wanted to come for an interview. Talk about really strange coincidences.

It turned out that they didn't know each other at all, and after being selected for a job with Correctional Services Canada, I returned my message to Bell saying that I would not be interested in the position after all. I then began my career as a civil servant, which led me to where I am today.

Sometimes I look back and wonder if I actually had gotten some of the jobs I had interviewed for, what it would be like, and if I would be any happier. I will list some of them near the end of this topic, and more importantly why I didn't get them, which is likely of benefit to us both!

If at some time in my life someone told me that I would be working in a Federal Prison, I would have assumed they were nuts. If at some time in my life someone told me that I would be incarcerated in a Federal Prison that I could more likely believe. In today's day and age, nothing is impossible.

It in fact seemed to be a turning point in my career because it took me from a career in Stationary Engineering, which was becoming a dying trade, into the field of Water and Wastewater. It is something that I have spent the last twenty years working, teaching and making a living from.

The other highlight of my three years there involved having the chance to play in the National Canadian Hockey Championship with the men's hockey team, which we won. Competing with teams from across Canada in a four-day event to decide the winner was quite an experience, both on and off the ice.

The sign that read "Come one, come all, come to the Newfie ball, where we have forty twenty sixers of Newfie Screech", still send shivers down my spine. You really need to develop a taste for that stuff.

When you work in Water and Sewage at a place like this, you can find some very interesting things, especially at the sewage plant!

Some of the more interesting involved two full size bed sheets, how I am still puzzled on how much effort and determination it takes to sit and flush, coil some more and flush again. I guess if you have a lot of time to kill, it could be a good way to do it. I myself would be afraid of clogging my system when I need it most.

Another strange one involved a taped banana, which I am not even going to get started on speculating about. That will be for everyone's benefit.

Prior to me getting there, they used to use money inside the pen to buy supplies. The inmates received a wage for working, which in turn bought cigarettes, candy, etc. The money had special markings, which could only be seen by putting it under a special light. The big thing then was if an inmate was caught with illegal money, or more than he could account for, then they would be punished. Therefore it was customary to flush the money down the system instead of being caught with it. There was a rumor that one employee found enough money to actually buy a new vehicle, but in my three years there, I think maybe it was more of a rumor than anything else.

There were two cases that stick out in my head that I remember like it was yesterday. The first involved the sewage plant being a stinky place to be, but low and behold the security guard's patrolling around the outside perimeter of the fence, just had to come down and see what was going on.

This one particular day involved a pretty young blonde girl who I see was getting her nerve up to come and see what was down over the hill. I could tell it was her first trip to the sewage plant, so I purposely made sure to get the garbage cans close enough to the road so that she could see the contents without having to leave the truck.

I also made sure to leave a pair of wet underwear on top of the pile. When she first seen them she gave out a shriek and commented on how gross that was. I simply replied that it was kind of gross but the job had definite benefits, because I knew she would ask what they were.

Then finally she did, in which I replied that I hadn't had to buy a pair of underwear since starting to work there. As I watched her mouth drop open, I also pointed out that the worse part was trying them on when they were wet. The final straw came when she started to change color and I said that it was easier to put them on wet than dry, because then they don't scratch your ass as much.

I tried not to let out a howl as her tires were spinning, the gravel flew, and her comments about me being "a sick person" was muffled by the gagging noises she was making. It wasn't right but damn it was funny!

My final story from my three years there comes from a conversation with an inmate who worked for us during the day. After talking with this individual for a few minutes, you could tell the elevator was jammed somewhere between floors and he was destined to be where he was until likely the day he died.

On this particular day though, he tried to start a conversation with me on how to sexually satisfy my wife. I kept telling him I was not interested in his techniques but he continued on until the best I could figure, it involved a chunk of tubing, some sucking on the tubing, and then some gentle blowing. Don't ask me why because the conversation ended at that point.

The rest of the day continued on and like a lot of days I stopped for a drink on the way home. After I finally arrived home, I found the urge that I had to share my story with my wife, which was normal for me.

I could see the look of disbelief on her face as I recounted the story in more detailed fashion for her, but I think that the climatic moment in the story came a few minutes after I was done telling it to her, when she asked why I was later than usual.

I only replied that I had to stop at the hardware store. That was followed by a look, a slap, and the words "you are sick".

Funny because that was the second time I had heard that phrase in a day!

Working at the pen would also introduce me to my new found fishing partner and overly helpful buddy, named Turner. He was quite unique in the fact that sometimes he would help me without me even asking for his help.

One time in particular was when he introduced me to the rifle range at work. He showed me how to shoot the AR15 rifle, which was extremely accurate at one hundred yards.

When at the range it was customary to shoot forty rounds with the rifle at a distance of one hundred yards. A person would shoot ten shots standing, ten sitting, ten kneeling, and finally ten lying down. All the shots would be toward a silhouette of a person, which had a series of rings that each scored different points. The closer the shots were placed to the centre of the target, the better the score.

The best possible score would be four hundred points, with 40 X, which meant that all the shots were put into an area as big as your fist.

On this particular day, someone else asked me to come and shoot to try and qualify for the rifle team, which shot in competitions at different Institutions.

After I had shot my forty rounds, the Instructor was overly impressed with my score and asked if I had wanted to join the team. The funny part was that I distinctly remember missing the target at least twice but somehow ended up with a better score than some of the long time team members had.

As I was pondering this miracle at the shooting range, I noticed another individual at the other end of the shooting area. This seemed a little strange because he was covered with some clothing that didn't make him clearly visible to us at the other end. So I decided to check it out a little closer.

I then asked the Instructor to check the number of holes in my target. It was strange that I could have fifty-three holes in my target when I had only fired forty! So of I headed to the other side of the shooting area.

When I arrived there I proceeded to go over and kick the pile of clothes that were covering up this mystery shooter. Once the chuckling subsided, I then asked him why he had shot my target, in which he replied that it didn't look like I was doing very well on my own.

This was just one example of how helpful he could be without asking. You will get to see more of him later in the book.

Three years after starting at the pen, I decided that I had had enough and it was time to move on again. Working with ammonia was uncomfortable and made me leave one job, but the atmosphere working there was more uncomfortable than that.

As I was looking for something new, my father presented me with a job posting from the local paper. It was close to home and in the field that I was working, so I applied. In the end it would turn out that I would spend the next fourteen years there.

This is where the part about being like a family, comes into play most of all. When I started there I was the oldest of three other employees, and the only one older was the boss.

When I said I was the oldest though, that would still only make me around twenty-six.

I was like the older brother with two younger sisters who were usually well behaved until the youngest brother got them wound up. The younger brother would be the "hell raiser" of the group, a rebel from day one.

And of course you would have the boss, who would play the part of the parent keeping us in line, and like any family the kids would always be good until the parents went away.

Before I elaborate too much, I must state that we always could handle a crisis if something came up. We were trained to be professional and that is how we conducted ourselves ninety-five percent of the time. With that said, this is the other five percent.

Many notable things happened over the years but here are some of the more eventful in no particular order.

I decided one day while our secretary was away that it would be funny to put clear plastic tape over the mouthpiece of her phone. It was quite comical to watch my co-workers trying to speak louder and louder into the phone anytime someone called. They eventually figured me out and started using the other phones. I unfortunately forgot about the phone by the end of the day.

I ended up being off sick for a day and when I got back I was informed by the boss that they had to have Bell telephone into to repair the phones because they had no volume when talking into them. It took me a minute to figure out what he was talking about until I suddenly remembered the Secretary's phone.

They kept me on the hook for a while until he told me quite sternly to "not try and do it again". She apparently had found the problem with the tape after a few minutes of hollering into the phone.

The most classic prank was when we had a mining engineer visiting the site to do some work with us for a couple of months. We had to set up a desk upstairs for him in the office and after awhile he was just settling in and getting used to the way we acted.

Unfortunately for him he didn't know that once he was there for a month, there was no more having to be on good behavior around him. I must say that his dry sense of humor was coming along well after spending more and more time alone with us. That was until he got a break in his schedule and returned home for a couple of weeks.

While he was away, I used to sit at his desk for coffee, and out of curiosity I would go through his desk to see what he left behind. I found some things like rubber bands, paper clips and a highlighter. All things that would be useful to make a trap if one was so inclined.

Each day as I sat there, I would try to assemble the objects into something useful. One day it came to me to wind the highlighter up with elastic bands, tape it to the drawer, and hold it down with the paper clips. Then when you opened the drawer it would make a rattling noise like something trying to escape from the drawer.

Meanwhile my younger co-workers would watch in amazement, wondering just what I was up to.

The day finally arrived when the engineer returned from holidays and was sitting at his desk. We were having coffee and he asked if anything new had happened while he was away. I had replied that they had torn down the building next door, which luckily they had just done. I also informed him of the problem we were having with rats since they tore the old building down. I said that they were showing up everywhere and to keep an eye out for them hiding.

Meanwhile Tick and Tack, my co-workers were staring at me trying to figure out where I got this rat story from, when it finally happened.

He opened the drawer to his desk, which ultimately tripped the rubber bands sending out this clanking noise like something trying to get out of his desk. Between the screaming, the look of terror, and the coffee flying across the desk, all hell broke loose.

I felt bad because he was as white as a ghost when I finally got him calmed down and I was just glad he didn't have a heart attack. I figured that any other pranks in the future shouldn't be as well set up as that one, even though the kids couldn't quit laughing at the memory of it.

That same room led to an embarrassing moment that involved us all one day, when we were sitting around having coffee.

The room was situated so that the entrance door was at my back, and I was facing the other two who were sitting at the desks in the office.

On this particular day, the boss was away, and the mice were about to play. Our Lab Technician was sitting in the boss's chair directly in front of me, when I came up with one of my witty comments. As I noticed her starting to laugh and the look on the other co-workers face starting to change, I decided to turn it up a few notches.

The more I performed the harder she laughed, with tears starting to form in the corner of her eyes. He on the other hand was grinning but with a hesitant look on his face. I continued on with my performance to the point where I was lecturing the filing cabinet. I gave it a swat and one of the drawers came opened. I then closed it and lectured it some more, and as I was doing so I had this sudden feeling of someone behind me.

That turned out to be true when I turned around, so I quickly adlibbed the line, "And what can we do for you?" without breaking stride.

I wish someone had informed me of the person who had come up the stairs behind me but it turned out he had a sense of humor and we were able to help him.

We had a policy of having to talk to a live person when we called in sick. I always thought that it was going overboard a little until the day they played back a message I had left two nights earlier when I had called in sick. The message itself was convincing enough to have won an Oscar for best performance, until the giggling in the background at the end of the message appeared.

Never giggle until after you have hung up the phone, especially at three in the morning!

A lot of the stories that found us getting
into trouble involved me working with my "hell
raiser" counterpart. This man had a mind of his
own and would only listen to the parts of a
suggestion from others that would directly
benefit him.

One case in question involved having to
collect samples along the river. The direction
from the boss was to stay off of the river because
it was not frozen. As I putted up through the
trail along the river on a four-wheeler, I looked
over to find "Hell Raiser" doing one of his death
defying stunts by driving up the centre of the
river on a snowmobile. I was shaking my head at
him, while he was waving to me.

It was on that same trip that we were
racing back to the shop. We were just getting
back to the shop when he again decided to
attempt fate with yet another stunt. As he blew
by me on the snowmobile, he forgot to calculate
his speed on the turn to the shop, and ended up in
a barrel role while the boss looked out the

window. I on the other hand, parked the ATV in the garage and headed up to the office.

As I hit the top of the stairs, I heard the boss holler at me to get into his office. He started to lecture me on the way I was driving the snowmobile, when I looked at him and questioned what he was talking about. He said that he had seen me out the window and that my counterpart had said that I was driving. I told him that he had better check again.

The one thing that was a given was my counterparts reputation was more distinguished than mine when it came to high risk maneuvers. It didn't take long to get things straightened out!

On another occasion we were traveling down a country road when a bee suddenly flew in my window and got caught inside my shirt. I screamed for him to stop as I worked to try and get the bee out without getting stung.

The more I wiggled the father down my shirt the bee slipped until he ended up getting down inside my pants. At this point I was outside the vehicle with my pants down around my ankles trying not to get stung in the privates.

As I was doing this, he decided that it would be prudent to snap some pictures with the portable camera we had with us. I was not only busy trying not to get stung but also trying to not end up as some slide show presentation at the Christmas party. Finally I got rid of the first pest and then threatened the second one about the use of the pictures.

One day for whatever reason, I found myself with some spare time on my hands while waiting for a task to finish running its course. I just happened to notice the Rolodex full of phone numbers sitting in front of me, when I got the great idea to put "Hell Raisers" name under each letter. Of course with each letter I would put his first name, followed by a descriptive phrase starting with that letter, and finally ending with his last name. It was a bit of a chore, but well worth it when he went to use the Rolodex the next time.

Of course he couldn't let that go, so he returned the favor the next time we were over that way. All was well until we had a breakdown at that plant and the boss had accompanied us there to help.

He decided to call for parts as we worked on fixing the problem. The unfortunate thing for us is that he didn't know the number so he reached for the Rolodex. That eventually lead to a meeting about leaving notes for each other in which he said that things were going to stop or else someone was going to pay.

As I left his office, I went downstairs and grabbed a cardboard box. On the side of it I wrote, "Oh yea, screw you Kelly" which I left for him to see. As he came down the stairs he let out a yelp and said to get rid of the box before he got in shit. He ended up throwing it over in the corner and about three weeks later the boss found it, which led to him getting in trouble.

You just have to love happy endings!

Finally, one of the most memorable times we had together was when we were on the sample run and found a blow up doll out along the highway. He was just in the process of moving at the time and I kept bugging him that it likely blew out of his truck on one of his trips.

That doll made the trip back to the shop where she was blown up, photographed, and later picked up and transported around the country as a conversation piece. To top it all off, after we finally got rid of the doll, we happened to find another one two weeks later in exactly the same spot. I just looked at him and asked if he was moving again?

Well that takes me up to present and rule number one in that category is to never talk about your present place of employment.

Hopefully they realize that all of this other stuff was worked out when I was just young, and that the foolish side of me has settled down. Well at least for now.

Some of the jobs that I missed out at in the interview process were:

Ontario Hydro when they asked me how to set the timing in a car, and I replied by turning the little black box.

My wife's uncle had informed me that I wouldn't have to climb right away with them, but when I checked out the newspaper the next week, the selected candidates had to climb up a steel tower and hang by their belt on the very first day. Missing that exercise didn't hurt my feelings at all!

I could have been the Manager of a Conservation Authority, except for answering the reason I wanted the job was to flood out my sister's house.

Finally, I could have been a Government Inspector on three different occasions but for some strange reason they had some concerns about me being able to be serious. Who would have thought?

Uncle Don, Cousin Ken & the Country

The first time I met Uncle Don was when my wife and I first started dating. We were headed to Belleville to my Christmas party when I had this strange thought that I was driving something the army would issue.

In the middle of the road was a dead raccoon. I figure thirty to forty pounds worth of raccoon. The muffler on my dad's car said it was more likely to be one hundred and fifty pounds after surveying the damage.

The whole event went something like this.

"God you look good tonight!" how did your day go?

"Oh pretty good, we were busy."

"Should be a fun night tonight, don't you think?"

"Do you think this outfit looks alright?"

"You look beautiful!"

"What's that big thing on the road? It looks like a dead raccoon!"

"It does, doesn't it?"

"Shouldn't you maybe try to swerve around it or something? It is pretty big?"

"Nah we'll be alright, this is a Dodge."

"Bwaaaaaaaaaghhhhhhhhhhh"

That is the sound a muffler makes when it gets torn completely off of the vehicle that you are driving. It turns out that even Dodges are not designed to overcome a big mass of dead animal lying in the middle of the road.

Possibly some four by four vehicle with good clearance might have had a chance to make it, but with a Dodge Monaco with very little clearance, it likely was not going to happen.

There we were just starting out on our voyage and we had encountered our first dilemma. I wanted to have a few drinks at the party and didn't want to attract any more attention than I needed.

The only thing the gets noticed more than a car with no muffler, is a fire truck with the sirens on. I could have possibly called in a fire while trying to get downtown with my dad's car, but that likely would have led to some type of jail time. Instead we decided to stop at Uncle Don's.

Now Uncle Don seemed to be this rough, grumpy, mean, "Tough as nails" guy on the outside, but hidden inside was a heart of gold. (Editor's note: After reading this part, he will likely not be talking to me for a bit, but now he has grandchildren and the secret is out)

It turned out that this was the one thing the girls could rely on.

Of course they new Uncle Don but I didn't. The only dilemma I had so far was coming up with an excuse of why I had tried to drive over forty pounds of dead animal with my dad's car. Now with having to meet Uncle Don, I had a new one.

It was time to play a thousand questions with Uncle Don. Unfortunately my wife's dad passed away when we first started dating, and at that time Uncle Don felt he should help look after his niece when it came to young lads and dating.

It was about that time that I realized something very special happened in my life. I was dating a girl who I would fall in love with, and unfortunately for her, she would become my wife.

The other thing was that I was introduced to living in the country, something you cannot really explain until it happens to you.

I imagine living in the country in Ontario equates to living in the Maritimes down east, where you have people looking after each other, and just making life simple.

Getting back to the story, I was in a "bit of frenzy" because I had a car with no muffler and we wanted to go to Belleville to the Christmas party, when Uncle Don said, "Take my car".

I replied that I thought that was great and Donna could drive.

He replied back, "Why do you not have a license?"

"Yes", I replied.

"Then why don't you want to drive?"

"You want a stranger driving your vehicle? I asked.

It was at this time that I noticed the look on his face. It was somewhere between the "I don't know why I shouldn't kick you in the ass" and the "He must be a "kid from town" kind of look"

My future wife smiled, took the keys and said to me to "come on". That was a very pivotal time in my life because having grown up in town and not experiencing rural living; it turned out to be a real eye opener.

Rural living would teach me how to relax, learn to love country music, and after numerous broken toes on my mother in laws feet, the ability to two-step. For those of you not into country music, that is the slow dance they do where they go two steps forward and one step back.

"NO, I DO NOT MEAN LINE DANCING!

That one still has me baffled. I think that dance was created in a washroom somewhere when the bathrooms were backed up. It was developed by twenty people all wanting to go to the bathroom, and who had to do something to get their mind off of their problems. On that day we witnessed the creation of line dancing.

When all was said and done, we made it to the Christmas party, had a great time and unknown to Uncle Don, my wife did drive home that night. That would turn out to be good for him and for me both.

Uncle Don would introduce me to a whole cast of characters over the years, that would leave memories that still make me chuckle every time I think about them.

One of those characters would have to be "Jungle Doug". I met Doug for the first time at Uncle Don's hunting camp. He had come in to visit and had a bottle of whisky already premixed with alcohol and mix.

Unfortunately I did not know this, because I watched him pour half of the contents of this bottle into his glass and drink it. I witnessed the same thing the second time. Three quarters out of the bottle with a hint of mix on the top. It didn't seem quite normal but I thought the man maybe liked his drinks strong.

It wasn't a problem until the booze that he brought was gone and Uncle Don told me to mix him a drink. Over to the counter, three quarters of a glass of "Seagram's 83", and topped up with a little mix.

A drink anyone should be proud of.

The first swallow ended up pretty well half way across the table, followed by the statement of "Are you trying to kill me?" It was at that time that I found out that the original bottle was premixed and not straight and from that point on we just poured normal drinks.

As the day progressed, I was able to pick up on Doug's ability to play people. I thought I was pretty good at it but Doug turned out to be the master.

He had headed outside to relieve himself by the closest tree. Afterward he decided to visit with one of the hounds that were tied up nearby, when all of a sudden he toppled over.

Don let out a holler, and three of the young lads proceeded out to pick up Doug and carry him back in. As he went by me he had his eyes closed, but then he opened one long enough to wink at me. When the boys finally set him down, he stood up and proclaimed, "Are you done boys?" as he walked over and poured another drink.

That was my first encounter with Doug, and one, which would also be just the "tip of the iceberg" as they say.

Another encounter with Doug would involve stopping at Uncle Don's garage. Don was trying to repair a faulty control for raising the window in the driver's door of his Suburban.

There was Uncle Don with his arms stuck inside the door right up to his armpits. On the outside was Doug in control of the whiskey. Uncle Don told me to get a drink and that he would be finished in a second.

Doug apparently thought that was too early for Don to be finished.

As Don struggled to remove the last bolt from this part, he handed the old part to Doug and asked for the new one.

Doug looked at me, looked at the part, smiled at me, and handed the old part back to Don.

Instead of telling Don it was the old part, he waited until he had at least one of the bolts done back up, when he said, "Are you sure that is the right one Don?"

As I noticed the shades of red on Don's face getting darker and darker, I knew it was a good time to step back and get out of the way.

When the old part came out this time, it made it all the way through the air to the outside wall of the garage across the building.

The last time I saw that look on his face was when we were taking down a trouble tree when Don had his tree contracting business.

He was only about sixty feet in the air up in a poplar tree when he inquired about the knot I was tying.

He asked if he needed to keep the other end of the rope when I was sending up the saw to him. I said "Don't you trust me?"

Well it was a little awkward when both ropes where on the ground with me, and he was in the tree empty handed. His question, "What are we going to do now?" was answered by silence.

When he returned to the ground, I asked if he would like me to tie the knot again. He just gave me that look, as if he wanted to tie a knot all right, but it would likely be around my neck!

I guess I never got to the point where Doug became known as "Jungle Doug". That would take place on the first day of deer hunting season when all of the people would be arriving all decked out in bright orange.

Doug arrived dressed in beige clothes and a safari hat.

From that day on, he would be known as "Jungle Doug" to everyone in the camp, possibly once I came up with the name. It just seemed fitting for the man and for the occasion.

Jungle Doug was not finished leaving memories in my mind on that day. He would head out into the sunrise the very next morning with his jungle hat on his head, and his jungle shirt draping down below his butt.

He would return at sunset with his jungle hat on his head and his jungle shirt cut even with his belt line on his pants.

"What to hell happened to your shirt?"

"You don't expect me to use leaves, do you?" was the reply.

Hunting season always allowed for two things. One was the hunt and the other was the socializing. I was always good at the second one, but later in life started to hate the first one. Who wanted to get up first thing in the morning after having so much fun the night before?

This leads me yet to another story about Jungle Doug.

It was the day after one of our long drawn out "Texas Hold-Em" tournaments. This morning Jungle Doug came down from the bedroom when I enquired as to where Doug was going to hunt that day.

He replied that he was going to hunt with Kenny on his watch.

I pointed out that Kenny because he was paralyzed from the waist down, hunts out of his truck.

Doug answered, "My point exactly"

No one new until late in the evening what exactly did happen that morning but I think it went something like this.

Kenny had this bad habit of fidgeting with his gun. This I found out when my wife and I were visiting Uncle Don and met Kenny in the laneway. It was pouring down rain and I was talking to Kenny through my window, which was opened just partially.

I said, "Why don't you have your window up?"

"There was a black snake in the drive way the other day" he replied.

"What"

"Well I was trying to get the gun out the window!"

"You shot the window out of your truck while trying to shoot a black snake?"

"Yea, but, but"

I looked at my wife and we started to laugh.

This is "Cousin Ken", who will need at least a whole chapter worth of pages to tell some of his antics.

Back to the story about "Jungle Doug" and "Cousin Ken" who were out sharing a watch.

Doug was trying to get some sleep after a long night of socializing while Ken decided to fidget with his rifle. That was all ok until somehow the rifle went off.

There went a 30-30 shell down through the floorboard of Kenny's vehicle, and then off the transmission and into the ground.

Meanwhile the whole time, while this was taking place, Doug was trying to sleep on the other side of the truck

I had to get a recount of what happened when they got back to the camp.

Apparently, Doug after getting his color back from a terrible shade of grey just mumbled the words, "Well…Did you get him Ken?"

There was very little response!

That would go down in the history books as just one of the most memorable times from the past. We were lucky that no one ever got hurt from it and that we had the chance for all of the characters to be in that place at one time.

"Jungle Doug" would move on to what people call a better place in life after he passed away, but his memories with us will live on forever especially at the camp.

I like to think if there is a better place than where we are now, it will likely be worth waiting for, because there are a lot of people like Doug that give us new memories everyday.

We just have to look for them and enjoy them while they are still here.

"Cousin Ken" who is Don's brother, was truly, an entity in his own time. Before I ever met the man, he was involved in a snowmobile accident that would take away his ability to walk but would not take away his ability to make an impression.

When my wife and I first started dating, we were at a dance in the nearby town we grew up in, called Marmora where Ken was also in attendance.

Ken was the only person I personally know, who could dance with his wheelchair.

Yes, I mean up on two wheels, with the front wheels off the floor, for the whole duration of the song. The crowd loved him, we loved him, everybody amazed at his talent.

Then I noticed a bit of a scam unfolding. "Cousin Ken" knows I love him like a brother, so I can go on with the story.

Here Ken was with the young girls wanting him to dance, up in the middle of the dance floor when someone hollered, "Ken is down!"

I turned to see Ken had upset the applecart, and was laying flat on his back in the middle of the floor. You are now likely thinking what kind of sadist I am for saying this was a scam. Kenny was down and out on the floor and I was being skeptical.

Then help started to conjure in to help save the man in distress. "Kenny, are you alright?" was heard as the people all flocked to his aid.

Someone said, "Is that not your girlfriend's uncle."

"Yes" I replied.

"Are you not going to help him?"

"Just watch for a minute, will you."

The fifteen or twenty people that finally up righted Kenny back into the chair also thought that he would feel better by buying him a drink. There he sat with a table full of whisky in front of him just because of one crash.

"Do you think he did that on purpose?" was the next question.

"I don't really know" I replied.

"It won't happen again will it?"

"Keep an eye on the table, and we will watch when the drinks are gone."

It was roughly about an hour and a half later when the next big spill took place. The one thing consistent about Kenny was the ability to make it look real every time it happened.

Then when I thought about it, the man just drank ten double whiskeys. There likely wasn't a lot of acting going on. Worst part was always the noise of his head hitting the floor when he dumped his chair. Unless he was taking lessons from the boys at the WWF on how to take a fall, it definitely had to hurt.

What was that saying, "NO pain, NO gain, and god why my head hurts so much?"

Anyhow with each big fall, came the attention, and with it, another round of drinks! You just have to love a man who is good at his craft. Houdini in a wheelchair!

One particular trip with Kenny that comes to mind was when Rob and I had Uncle

Don's truck, and we were heading to the hunting camp.

I know, "Who the hell is Rob?"

Rob would be the young lad that I met in high school and who was likely my best friend until I fell in love with his sister. She would ultimately become my "only best friend".

Rob would also be the oldest and the only son of Bob and Marie, followed by my wife Donna, and their sisters Beth, and Leanne.

On this particular day, we were headed to the hunting camp with Kenny, and for whatever reason he did not have his chair. We got to the camp when we realized that if we were going to spend the night, we would need some supplies.

We asked Ken if he would be alright until we ran out to the house nearby, got some supplies, and came right back. Should only be twenty minutes top. Kenny of course agreed.

We left Kenny with four pints of beer and a twenty-six-ounce bottle of whiskey, and sat him in a chair near the table. It was late March and quite warm in the daytime.

When we got out of the camp, uncle Don decided that he would like to come with us, but realizing that we were short on booze, sent us to the bootlegger.

For those of you unfamiliar with the bootlegger, he or she was the person that would sell you alcohol after hours when the stores were closed, or to people that looked old enough to buy it at an extremely increased price!

One very important thing to remember is to make sure that the bootlegger is actually a bootlegger before you start dealing with them.

This brings up the case of my friend Rick and I, going to the bootlegger in a small town not far from us. In the days my dad traveled there, it always had something to do with the store.

I thought it was in the store, but as I would find out the correct phrase was "behind the store". Also about fifty some years had passed since dad had used the bootlegger before we went looking for her at the same spot.

It didn't matter because I told Rick to wait out front of the store and I would go in and negotiate.

"Could I help you sir?"

"Go ahead and finish with the other couple first." I replied.

As the other people left, the woman looked quite pleased with my courtesy, and asked, "What can I get you?"

"I need a big bottle of whiskey"

"You need what?"

"I need a bottle, a jug…a jug of whiskey?"

"We don't sell liquor here!"

"You are the bootlegger, aren't you?"

As she was reaching for the broom and coming towards me, I ran for the truck.

Rick said "where is the booze?'

"Drive, just drive, she is not a bootlegger" was my reply.

After some investigative inquiries in town, I found out that the bootlegger actually was behind the store and not in the store. I also found out that the people that bought the store were quite religious and likely didn't even deal with the bootlegger.

Kenny meanwhile was back at the camp without a chair. Rob and I had picked up the booze at a more local, and known bootlegger, and had headed back to get uncle Don.

My concerns were that it was getting cold and Kenny had no way of getting around.

Apparently that old saying "Where there is a will, there is a way" came into play.

Kenny not only had the fire going, he had consumed all four pints of beer and three quarters of the forty ounce bottle of whiskey.

We could have left him there for a week and the man would have trapped mice to survive.

I guess that is why when I here the word "disabled" that it only maybe applies to a person's frame of mind. I have met many people over the years who have had unfortunate things happen to them but who still fit into everyday life better than people that never had to deal with hardship.

"I don't feel well because I have a cold"

Get off your ass long enough to go over and talk to those people. They are the ones that have a right to complain, but do they?

No, because they are survivors and they still want to participate in this great thing we call life!

To all those people that put forth that effort everyday, I commend you for showing the rest of us what life is really all about.

Living in the country always brought about some very strange things.

I remember lying in bed dreaming about hearing horses running down a road when I suddenly realized that I had the bedroom window open, and I wasn't asleep. I woke up my wife and turned on the outside lights to see these horses all in my front yard which meant a phone call to Harry my neighbor to come and get them.

I didn't mind the horses on my front lawn, but the thought of someone hitting them on the road made me shiver. Sure enough Harry and his wife and daughters arrived in the middle of the night to try and get them corralled back to where they had broken.

The other thing I used to love was the sound of deer blowing when they are trying to warn other deer of danger. Unless you have heard it before, you would not pick up on it. It sounds like a sharp whistle sound that makes the hair on the back of your neck stands up.

My old dog, "Sammy" would sleep outside on our deck. Before we had built our house, it used to be known as a famous deer crossing as the deer would come down from the rocks and head out into the fields to graze.

I would be lying in bed half asleep, when the deer would try to sneak down between our house and Grandma's.

No we haven't talked about her yet, but we will.

The deer would be just about through their course when one of them would pick up the scent of the dog on the step. It would then let out that sharp shrill sound that would wake me from a dead sleep.

At first I would be ticked at being startled by the sound but then I would have this smile come over my face knowing what had just taken place. We had built a house in their domain, but somehow we all came to co-habitat even with the addition of the dog.

I still remember the time the girls were waiting to get on the school bus when all of a sudden a young buck, who is a male deer, not some scrapping young lad, came running up through the field across the road.

It had a broken antler on one side of its head and was going to come directly up the driveway to the astonishment of the two kids. Suddenly it retrieved its bearings and came to a dead stop, looking across the road at us.

The girls looked at me, I looked at the deer, and we all began to laugh as the deer turned and headed back across the field in the opposite direction.

Those were the times in my life that I felt privileged to be able to raise my kids in the country. The ability to exchange glances with wildlife and to intermingle with them was something a lot of people never get to enjoy!

Then there was the time with the raccoon. This time it wasn't dead on the road, but in our house.

My wife and I were in bed when all of a sudden there was the sound of beer bottles being knocked over. I didn't have a case for them so I would stack the bottles in the corner by the sliding door in our dining room.

I said to my wife that it was likely one of the kids.

She pointed out that the kids weren't home.

I told her "Go check it out."

I cannot print what she said back.

I said that maybe it was just our imagination until I heard all of the beer bottles being knocked over.

We carefully came out of the bedroom to find the screen on the sliding glass door open about a foot.

It meant that there was either a very noisy, skinny burglar in the house, or a wild animal.

Our kitchen and dining room consisted of an open concept with an island in the center of the kitchen. Just off the kitchen was a set of stairs, the only set of stairs, entering down into the basement.

I said to my wife that I would check the island, while she checked the basement,

I cannot print what she said next.

Normally the island in your kitchen would not scare you, unless of course there is an animal hiding behind it. Together we went around the island and were debating on whom, if anybody was going to go downstairs and check the basement.

Finally I heard a noise on the deck outside, and went out to find an oversized raccoon slinking away from underneath the deck. He headed off into the woods carrying a couple of beer bottles with him. Ok, he didn't have any beer bottles with him, but it did mean that I didn't have to check downstairs.

My exchanges with nature outside of the house were a lot more enjoyable than the ones inside. If I want to see you, I will come out or go to a zoo. Please do not come into the house!

Camping, Cottages and Hunt Camps

The one thing I have learned over the years is that people that come from different places are not really different.

I use the following example, which compares people who live and work in the city to people who live and work in a rural setting.

The people in the city work all their lives so that they can purchase a cottage somewhere peaceful. In the meantime they get a bunch of friends together and go camping in the wilderness while on vacation.

The people that live in the rural areas work all their lives so that they may someday buy a cottage. They then sell it for five times what they paid, to someone from the city that needs it more than they do. They then in turn build a hunting camp.

Now I know you are asking yourself what is the difference between camping, owning a cottage, and having a hunting camp. All are out in the middle of the woods, or near a lake, usually away from a lot of neighbors or activity.

So the big thing becomes ownership. If you own the cottage or the hunting camp you will do things to keep it in good shape. You will do the necessary chores to make the place look nice and to keep it livable.

If you are visiting either one, or if you are camping, then there will be this demon inside you that takes your sole, usually just prior to you arriving there.

It will make you act like you always wanted to at the office Christmas party but were always afraid to. You will drink enough alcohol and act up to the point where you start speaking languages that "you" don't even understand. Then you will hate everybody and then love everybody all in the same weekend.

The difference is that no one ever used to take camera phones with them in the old days. There were only the horror stories you had to worry about, but not any physical footage on tape.

I remember a particular fishing trip with the boys to my good friend Ron's cottage. The demon hit me about the time I left the house and got in the van.

After drinking all of the way back to the cottage, which is still allowed in Canada, if traveling on back roads and you are not driving. This law has not thoroughly been tested after meeting up with an Ontario Provincial Police officer, so I caution you to its authenticity.

This is knowledge that I have been given by my elders over the years when asking the question, "Are you supposed to be drinking on the way to the camp?"

So it might be wise to deny having any thing in the vehicle if you get stopped. It usually isn't a good time to start an "open" discussion, especially with "open" liquor in the car.

Once inside the cottage we decided to have a few more drinks, visit and relax.   At that time my youngest daughter was just being toilet trained, and she had a habit to drop her pants to her ankles, announce to the room that she had to go, and head off to the bathroom.

People find that cute when you are a toddler, but people find it hilarious if you are over thirty and do the same thing while at the cottage.

Of course once I got a laugh from that, I decided to do it the rest of the night, much to everyone's amusement.

The next morning when I got up and the demon was still sleeping, I was just starting to recount some of the night before, when one of the boys brought up the pants around the ankles routine.

He commented on how funny it was, especially when Gord and Bernie had stopped by.

Now Gord and Bernie were also very good friends of mine, so this wouldn't have been too bad except for Bernie was Gord's wife.

So I asked the question, "Gord and Bernie were here?

This was right about that time that the video in my head pictured them sitting at the table laughing. I realized that this definitely was going to make for a long day!

I fretted for quite awhile until I met them again and kept apologizing for the event that night. They just kept laughing and laughing and laughing until I eventually came up with this demon scenario.

At least with cottages there are usually some neighbors or people around somewhere nearby. That isn't the same with hunting camps.

Hunting camps are usually full of testosterone filled men who want to return to a caveman style way of living. They want to build fires, read girly magazines and shoot things, which of course wasn't that popular in the day of the caveman for lack of guns not being invented yet.

They had to build the wheel so that it would lead to the car, so I guess you didn't need to build the gun until you wanted to steal the car. Who said that evolution didn't make sense?

As for the girly magazines, it is easier to carry a folded up magazine to the outhouse with you then it is to try and get a stone tablet through the doorway.

Maybe that is why some of the original outhouses had two seats, so that you would have someone to help with the stone tablet, but didn't do much for your privacy.

The main focus at hunting camps is of course to go hunting for wild game. The trick is to survive the whole week without wanting to hunt each other.

Usually depending on the age of your group, you will end up with two distinct groups and a third independent group.

You will have the old guys who get up earlier and go to bed early at night. They have a strict regiment and they do not like noise when they are trying to sleep at night.

You then have the young lads who want to stay up late and hate getting up in the morning. They do not like noise when they are trying to sleep in as long as they can in the morning.

You then have the passive, trouble-making group who can do both but are usually being too creative to go to bed at night or to get up in the morning.

I have always found myself to be a passive, creative person!

That is also why I have a shirt with ten names on the front saying these are the camps that I belonged to. It is the same shirt that has eleven names on the back saying these are the camps I have been kicked out of.

The eleventh name came while visiting friends and having a discussion why they should let me into their camp. On the way out the door they told me to add their name to my shirt. I said, "To the front so I am in?" They replied, "No, to the back, you are out!"

Over the years though, I have been able to go back and visit these camps and do what I do best, which is visit! My father hunted for years and then eventually lost interest. I think I am becoming more like him everyday.

Hunting Camps and Fishing Trips

I have mentioned some stories already about different things that had happened over the years at hunting camps, where I have met some very unique individuals. But the story would not be complete until I told you some of the other interesting things that have happened to me along the way. So if you are ready, here we go!

I have had people tell me that what I wanted was not a hunting camp to go to, but rather a lodge or resort. That could be very well true because once I get to a camp and start drinking, I really don't like doing a lot of chores the next day. I would much rather go in before hunting season and try to have as much done as possible to allow rest periods between drinking binges.

It doesn't seem to matter what camp you go to, each one has its own set of characters and each one seems to have one dog that sort of controls things. I have witnessed three different cases in particular where dogs had control of the camp and the story goes something like this:

The first one was a big black lab named Goober, who apparently had a free pass to stay in the camp. His claim to fame was that he had a favorite chair in the camp, and apparently when he got tired he wanted in it. It didn't matter if you were sitting in his chair; he would come and work you over until you got out of it.

I happened to be sitting in it one afternoon when he decided it was time for a nap. I was also tired so I decided that I was not going to move. He then proceeded to come over and put his head in my lap, which seemed cute at the time. He then had his head behind my back, then his shoulders, and finally his ass. Then all I could feel were the four paws pushing me out as I fell off of the chair onto the floor, much to the amusement of everyone watching.

The second one also involved a dog-named Goober, but this one was more the size of a small racehorse. We came across him while hunting in the woods, and when we started back to the camp he followed us. I noticed the name on the tag, so I told my partner Hudson to tie up the dog, while I poured us a drink and called the owner.

I was watching out the window as Hudson came strolling along with Goober about two feet behind. I said to him that I thought I told him to tie up the damn dog in which he replied that he had. I then told him to look behind him and maybe try again.

Off they went and as I finished leaving a message for the owner, I returned to the window to see the return of Hudson with good old Goober again only a couple of feet behind. I asked my friend if he had failed knot tying in school by any chance and decided that I might better do this task myself.

I then took old Goober with me over to the tree and proceeded to tie him up myself. I then watched as he took about three bites of the rope we had, and again began walking over to the house. I then decided it would be easier to take Goober home than to try and keep him there. So I called the owner stating that we would bring him home because we didn't have enough rope to keep him tied up.

When we did get him home, I see his regular chain was made of a logging chain tied to his doghouse. I figured that would have to slow him down a bit.

The third dog was a little beagle that reminded me of a mailbox on wheels. He had this uncanny act to be playing in the middle of the room and if he noticed someone looking at him, he would take off towards them and hurl himself through the air directly into them. I made the mistake of looking his way once I had laid down in bed, which led to an all out assault.

Seeing he was just a pup they would leave him at the camp during the hunt because they were afraid of him taking off. I came back first the one day, so I took him off his leash and brought him inside the camp. Somewhere by the time I had started breakfast for the boys and their return to the camp, he had demolished a full size push broom, a box of shells, and a wayward toque someone had left lying around. The owners of the shells and the toque were not impressed when they got back, but I couldn't quit chuckling long enough to tell them what had happened.

As for my time at the hunt camps, somebody wanting to drink with me at different times of the day usually plagued me, in which I tried to oblige. This one particular night was quite long and when everyone was up the next morning, I was cornered by one of the older lads who wanted to know where I was going to hunt.

My reply was the "tree stand", in which they said that they didn't have a tree stand. I said that we did, and that all they had to do was to go through the kitchen into the bedroom, turn right and go up three steps to the tree stand.

They then informed me that it was my bunk and not a tree stand, in which I replied, "Exactly".

That was the same camp where I was just about killed in the middle of the night by my fellow hunters. They said it was my fault but as I recall it wasn't all completely my fault, because I did have a little help.

You see when I am drinking I have this urge during the middle of the night to have to go to the bathroom. Just like clock work, the same time every night, I am up and out of bed and heading outside to go the bathroom. It is not that big of a deal because you just head outside the back door and let her go.

Unfortunately for me I sometimes think too much. On the very first night this happened, I woke up and climbed down from my bunk onto the floor where I found myself surrounded by a room full of snoring people. It would be roughly about sixteen people in a room, maybe twenty by twenty feet. I think you get the picture.

For some strange reason, I suddenly found myself having the urge to holler "Fire in the pug mill" while standing in the middle of the room. It would have been ok if I had of kept it as an urge, instead of acting on it.

As I returned from outside after going to the bathroom, I was greeted by some hostile campers who did not find the prank as humorous as I had. They even threatened me with some type of beating, which I wrote off as them not having enough sleep and just being grumpy.

Well on night two at the same time as the night before, I was wide-awake again. This time though I made my way quietly across the floor without waking any of my fellow campers. Until of course the urge came back again, and I let another "Fire in the pug mill". This time though I was also running outside and made sure I stayed there long enough for everyone to get back to sleep, or at least most of them. Again there were grumblings of a beating if I didn't shut up and let them sleep.

The third night, I was scared to get out of bed, but I had to go to the bathroom again. As I found myself in the centre of the floor, the urge returned, only to be overshadowed by the visions of being beaten by the angry mob. I carefully worked my way to the back door of the building and quietly opened the door as to make sure and not wake anyone.

There on the other side of the door was a lost Beagle who jumped towards me barking his head off. I in turn let out one of the loudest screams that anyone could have heard. It wasn't long before the lynch mob was up and ready to kill me. I tried to plead my case about the lost dog, but like in the story of the "man who cried wolf", I wasn't getting anywhere.

The only thing that saved me was that someone else went to go outside and the Beagle started up again. Once they checked out my story they let me off, but with a warning to not have any more fires in the pug mill for the rest of the week.

At another camp, something happened to me on the first Saturday when we had just arrived at the camp. We were there for the week and now that we had settled in, I thought it was a good time to celebrate. The only problem was that I noticed things were starting to close in and it was still daylight outside. Someone suggested that maybe I should have a sleep and then I would be ready for the big Saturday night party. That turned out to be a good idea.

The only problem with that idea seemed to be when I tried to wake up. I opened my eyes and noticed it was dark outside but that wasn't the problem. The problem was that I thought I had just seen a clown crawling through the window of the camp. To make it worse, a monkey was following the clown. I decided to give up.

I got up and packed my bags and headed out to the living room at the camp, where someone asked me what I was doing. I replied that I was going home. When they asked why, I told them about the clown and the monkey coming through the window.

To make matters worse, the clown, the monkey, Raggedy Ann and Charlie Chaplin were all sitting in the living room of the camp as I was telling my story. I then had to ask, "Does anyone else see them?"

Then someone replied that the women had got dressed up and came into the camp for Halloween, which made me feel quite relieved. I knew it was going to be too long a week to stay if that kind of stuff was happening on the first day without an explanation!

On one other occasion, I decided to go into the camp for a duck hunt by myself. It involved hunting off the shoreline where I would sit by a big pine tree, have a beer sitting beside me, and watch for ducks to fly by. This was usually a nice quiet, peaceful, return to nature.

This particular night was really slow until a lone duck was heading down the creek towards me. I took a bead on him and pulled the trigger of my twelve gauge shot gun. I could not see for the branches of the tree and the duck had been right at the end of the range for my gun, so I assumed that I had missed.

Then as I sat down beside my beer, I heard this crashing noise coming down through the trees. It was the duck travelling at around forty miles per hour, which hit the ground with a big thud. Twelve inches away from me!

On the right my beer, on the left the duck, and in the middle, my very pale colored face. It was the only time in history where the search party would have found a man with a broken neck, sitting between a half full beer, and a dead duck. The only "fowl play" being the duck killed the man out of pure spite. I had seen a duck land close to me before, but that was way to close, especially when you are all by yourself.

The other half of my time was usually spent fishing. I would fish in the summer with my partner Turner doing some tournaments, and spend the winter, living at the "Fish Hut."

We would share some great fishing stories about fish huts, but one I remember having the most fun with, involved the Bertrand brothers telling me they had a muskrat come up the hole of their fish hut. I just couldn't let this one go, and I made many good suggestions on how to avoid this problem in the future. A couple of suggestions were that they should not have cattails around the windows of their fish hut, and that if they couldn't get it level, they possibly had it sitting on a muskrat house.

While sitting in my own fish hut one day, I had a visitor stop by who had walked across most of the lake. I asked if he would like a beer and started up a conversation about how they made out in deer season. His reply was, "Just because we are parked on the north side of the road, doesn't mean we are hunting on the north side of the road". I wrote that response off to frost bite, chugged my beer and said that I had to leave. Maybe the next visitor will be more coherent, but remember this is ice fishing.

As for my fishing partner Turner, he was one of the most dedicated, hard working fishermen there was. He would try all types of bait, cast his little heart out, and spend all his time scouting. He then of course would pick up me when he needed to catch fish.

Actually I couldn't hold a candle to him, but for some strange reason I always had luck on my side. Especially if fishing for big bass that liked to take their time feeding. My rubber dew worm with a special twist, followed by a beer and a sandwich, would truly piss him off every time I pulled in a big fish. I think the thought of him casting and casting, and me sitting there with my line drifting in the water, drinking my beer and nibbling on my sandwich was just too much for him to bear, and eventually he would fire me from the fishing team.

It was either that, or possibly it was I getting sick over the side of the boat during the whole duration of one tournament that did it. If I had of been him, I would have tried to find another partner long before he did. All in all we did quite well in the tournaments we did go in.

Fishing in the summer with Turner was one thing, but fishing in the winter with him was the complete opposite. It was like letting a mad man out of the asylum. I have seen him put wood over the top of the stovepipe outside the fish hut to smoke people out from inside.

I have seen him tie a mannequin's hand to the end of my line while I was outside the hut and I have seen him hide a man's pole on top of the hut, and tell him that that a big pike had likely pulled it through the hole in the ice.

He has even taken a brand new person out ice fishing and drilled two holes in one area and another two holes quite a distance away. He would explain that it makes for a better chance to catch fish and that they would have to sit by the first set of holes and monitor the second set with the use of little red flags. He would say that if the flags moved, they would have to run over to the lines and feel if a fish was tugging on them.

What he didn't explain was that he was going to run some clear fishing line above the ice from the far set of lines to where they were sitting. The purpose was that to the average eye you could not see this line unless you actually tripped over it.

He then would wait until the young lad had just sat down, and then he would reach down and give the line a tug. This of course would get the red flag waving and result in the young lad having to run over to the lines to check.

He would do this again and again until finally the young lad would eventually trip over the line. The man was way too creative!

My final fish hut story involves heading to the lake on a Sunday morning. I got up first thing in the morning and tried to sneak out without waking up my wife. She knew I was going fishing, but the problem was I was extremely hung over, and I was trying to smuggle some booze out of the fridge without waking her up.

As I tried to get four bottles of beer out of the fridge at once, they started to clank together. I reminded them that they had been my best friends the night before, and that it was no time to turn on me. Finally I had my supplies loaded and I headed down to the lake.

When I arrived, I got the lines set up, the fire going, and contemplated what to have to drink. I then remembered that I had some whiskey and some pop left from the night before, so I decided to have a shot. Then put the radio on and the morning was going to be good.

That is when things took a turn for the worse. I was just about to have my first drink, when I heard something "MOO" outside. I shook my head and took a drink. I went to have a second drink, when I heard "MOO" again. I shook my head the second time. When I heard the third "MOO", I finally said that enough was enough. I went to the door of the hut and opened it up to find a cow and a dog standing on the ice together.

Seeing we live in the country, I could see a cow on shore happening, but a cow on the ice was hard to believe. One traveling with a dog was even harder to believe. So I went back in the hut. It wasn't since the clowns coming through the windows at the hunting camp that I had experienced a day like this.

I tried one more drink thinking it would all go away, only to hear yet another "MOO". I pushed my drink to the side and put my head down on the table. I had given up!

Awhile later I heard a snowmobile coming to the shack and someone stopped to visit. When they asked how I was, I told them about the cow and the dog. They informed that there was actually a cow and a dog. Well to be more exact a bull and a dog, and the bull's name was Bob.

"Bob" the bull and his sidekick dog would travel all over the place like a pair of hounds. They even headed into town once before their owner could catch them. Once I heard the story, I asked to have my rye back and the day began being well again, now that I knew who to hell Bob was.

The last time I heard of Bob the bull was when he ended up in the neighbor's custom-built flowerbed and completely ate the work of some designer. It was shortly after that incident that the only trace of Bob around was the smell of rib eye's cooking on the barbeque down the road. I even think his travelling partner got to eat the scraps left over.

Edward "P"

I don't really know for sure when I met Edward "P" for the first time or exactly where it was. If I had to venture a guess though, it would have been at his dad's shop or at our local meeting spot.

His dad owned a local automotive parts supply store in which he would eventually take over later in life.

The other local meeting spot I cannot name because of copyright laws, so for now we will just call it the "Gegion".

That it how it is pronounced when you are a little kid and someone asks where your dad is, or it is also how it is pronounced when you are gone all afternoon and your wife wants to know where you have been instead of doing the chores assigned to you.

Copyright or not, I have been a member of the Royal Canadian Legion for over the last twenty-five years and proudly want to thank all the veterans from the past, the present and the future for allowing us to live in the free country that we do, and to live the lives we have been given.

The Legion has changed over the years that I have been a member with a steady decline in members, mainly due to age. I hope and pray that the youth of today become aware of the importance of this great monument that exists that not only pays tribute to the people that have kept us safe, but also helps the community in so many ways today.

Back to Edward "P" and how we met. I am sure it was over some part I needed for my ever-struggling vehicles, or maybe after work over some long-winded story.

I think why we hit it off at the start, was that he was as foolish as I was, and could likely out fib me during story telling period.

One of the times I remember at the start, took place while sitting side by side at the bar with some other patrons. I had just ordered another beer when Phoebe, the tiny but feisty bartender brought it over.

I opened it up and took a swig. "Yuck, whoa, what is a matter with this?" I replied.

"What is a matter dear?" Phoebe asked.

"Flat" I replied.

"I will get you another one," she said.

"What's wrong with it?" Edward "P" piped in for no apparent reason.

"It's flat stupid, where you not listening?"

A shrug of his head and the rolling of his eyes met my answer.

"Try it then stupid, if you don't believe me!" I suggested.

He then took a big swallow and deliberately looked at Phoebe and myself and pronounced, "It tastes fine to me!"

Phoebe countered with "I will get you a new one anyway."

"Thanks Phoebe" I replied.

Then there was a minute of silence before Edward "P" decided to tell me, "Why don't you try mine"

"You actually want me to try yours?" I replied.

"Yes" he replied.

"Ok, give it to me!"

It was at this point and time that I realized that Edward "P" and I were going to be good friends. Not only because we both liked to drink, gamble, and visit, but more importantly for a smart ass to be able to upstage another smart-ass, as they say on the Visa commercial, is "PRICELESS".

I proceeded to pick up his full glass, put it to my mouth, tilted my head back, and chugged the whole thing!

I then turned to his bewildered looking face to proclaim, "No yours was fine!"

His reaction and the words he used unfortunately cannot be printed, but damn it was funny. Everyone at the bar including myself enjoyed that moment, but I did feel guilty enough that I bought him another beer.

Then there was the time that someone decided that we were not only entertaining enough to our fellow comrades at the bar, but that Edward "P" and I should go visiting to the

United States of America, which likely lead to the border crossing rules in place today.

It was an annual trip that a group makes to beautiful Ann Arbor, Michigan to attend the NASCAR race at Michigan International Speedway.

The trip was a great idea. I brought my wife with me to keep me in line but Edward's wife Sherry, for some reason sent him on his own, which I would eventually see why.

I like to act up and act foolish in my own surroundings, but when you get me away from the comfort of home, and visiting in a different country, I then become quiet as a church mouse.

Edward "P" apparently missed out on the church mouse philosophy because he didn't realize or care that we were in a different country.

I should have clued in when he said, "I can't believe how much U.S. change you get down here?"

I replied, "We are in the United States."

It didn't take him long to make friends once we arrived at our motel and somehow he became involved in part of an annual plumbers convention.

I realized that somehow I would have to try and be some kind of chaperone for him for the weekend but I also had to look after myself, which I remembered is why my wife was with me. Possibly she could look after the two of us if need be.

I knew the only way that I could even suggest that was to set up a shopping trip for the women, while Edward "P", me and Dan the organizer of the trip went golfing.

That of course seemed like another good idea at the start.

Once we finally decided and found a golf course to play, we had to make reservations, which we luckily got in on a beautiful course just outside of Ann Arbor.

I like to play golf and I will cheat a little bit if my ball is not in the right place.

We like to say a mulligan per nine holes is a good rule, but I don't like going outside that because you do not know how you really played at the end of the day.

Well the first time I saw Edward "P" after teeing off on the first hole was when he knocked his ball in the woods. He said that he could play his ball from where it laid, and as Dan and I made our way down the fairway, we could catch glimpses of Edward "P" through the branches.

The last time I saw Edward "P" on the first hole was when he knocked his ball out of the woods onto the green.

I said to Dan, "Give me a six."

"I had a five", Dan replied.

"Give me a six" was the response from Edward "P" much to the astonished look on our faces.

"How could you have a six? You were in the woods longer than most bears over winter!"

Edward "P" than used the phrase "Oh yea" "Screw you Kelly" which we will use for literary purposes and to keep the book fairly clean.

It would become the fuel for the fire for the weekend. I would fire the insult, and he would fire the same comeback, and the people on the trip would have a ball.

On the way to the track I noticed a heavily wooded area in which I stated "There is your fairway Edward "P", which led to his normal boisterous reply.

It was one of those trips that you can never recreate, no matter what you do or who is involved.

Golfing with these two on some separate occasions on these trips, bring back memories that men can actually "piss their pants" from laughing so hard if they can't find a place to go.

The first happened on another course where Dan was having the game of his life, being two under par after six holes. It was a long par three and Dan had out a driver. He went to swing as I commented on how well he was doing, and all hell broke loose.

The ball went way to the right, the head of the club came off the shaft and went flying into the woods to the left, and Edward "P" was standing by the ball washer, killing himself laughing, but also yelling "I got to go pee, I got to go pee!" while dancing like one of your kids at the shopping mall.

There we were, Dan staring into the woods with amazement, Edward "P" laughing and dancing, and me roaring my head off while not quite sure if it was over the club or Edward "P".

The same day when I thought to myself that nothing would ever come close to that event, one more thing happened.

Dan tended to be impatient when it came to waiting for people to play their ball, so he always seemed to be ahead.

I said that Edward "P" was behind him in the fairway and was getting ready to shoot, but he did not want to wait.

Dan was in the middle of his backswing when Edward "P's" ball came bouncing through his legs, which made me start giggling and dancing looking for a spot to go.

The award for the most memorable event that took place in the United States involved a Saturday night after everyone returned from the Bush race.

Everyone was in a party mood and they were down in the pool area, with people mingling with each other from all over the place.

I was keeping a particular eye on my partner Edward "P" when I noticed he was heading to the pool for a swim. There were all kinds of people in the pool area and of particular mention; there were two girls in the hot tub adjacent to the pool.

Normally two girls in a hot tub wasn't something to mention, but when they started necking in front of everyone, I knew Edward "P" had noticed.

Of course when I brought it to his attention, he informed me that it didn't really do anything for him.

Then he got out of the pool. As he started up the steps, I noticed that he had a certain condition that probably the hotel could have used. That was if they needed to hang a flag on something in case one of their flagpoles was down for repair.

I couldn't resist asking, "So the girls in the hot tub didn't do anything for you?"

With a shrug, and a frown he replied, "No, what makes you think that?"

I replied "Full mast!"

"What's full mast?"

"Look down stupid!"

There was a little shriek, followed with some turning red, and more giggling as he headed back down into the pool until the condition returned to normal.

Edward had already won my respect for being a legend by what he had accomplished earlier in life. I had smashed up two vehicles, one while sleeping when sober, and the other while trying to sleep when drinking. Neither one was something that I was proud of.

145

Edward "P" held the award though for not stopping for the police on a snowmobile while being chased by a police car.

The first award came when he used his intuition and lost the police by going through a field but continued on to return to his home at which they were waiting.

The second, more monumental award came when he decided to run them the second time. He took off down the street and ended up rolling the snowmobile just after he gave the police "the finger."

I still imagine the police wake up in the middle of the night laughing remembering that story. It's just too bad we didn't have "You tube" back then. Edward "P" would have been famous!

Edward "P" didn't get his sense of humor, his compassion to help others, or his kindness from anywhere strange. His father started their family business and his mother was a wonderful schoolteacher who would retire as Principal.

Unfortunately his father left us this year after a long, tedious battle, but in doing so he left many fond memories to his friends, family and especially to us at the Legion in Madoc.

The one classic tale that I will always remember involved one of their more outspoken customers, who always had something to say. On this particular day the customer walked in and looked at their big golden lab lying on the floor with his leg over his head, cleaning himself.

He said to Edward's father, "Would I ever like to be able to do that."

Without looking up from his paper work Bob replied, "You better ask him first!"

It is truly a classic story from another very good friend that I was fortunate to get to know and spend some time with over the years.

His legend, as will Edward "P", will live on with their children for years to come.

Edward's son now lives with and shares a house with my daughter and five others, while away at College. So you can only just imagine what stories they will have to tell!

Nellie and the Barbeque

It was a beautiful spring day when my wife shouted at me that my daughter needed my help. I was a little confused because she was only home on the weekends from college, and usually didn't have a lot of free time available for her dad.

It turned out that because she was a student living away from home all the time, she apparently didn't ever get to eat steak. That was funny because since we had a child in college, we seemed to find the same thing.

It turned out the problem existed with the barbeque. We apparently hadn't used it in quite awhile, because over the winter there seemed to be some mice move in. That seemed funny because we hadn't even advertised the barbeque as being "vacant".

I only go two hundred and forty pounds on this given day, and I am not going to, I repeat, not going to take on these mice. So I call on Nellie, my good old faithful cat.

I knew I had to call in a favor, seeing I have had to pay room and board for Nellie since she wandered in off the old country road, back when one of the girls were having a birthday party.

When it comes to men vs. mice, you leave it to the professionals. Apparently the mice moved in some time after we quit using the barbeque.

With two of our schedules, and us working it just didn't get used, and there was not a big requirement to warm up fast food on the barbeque, once someone brings it home.

I arrived on the scene to find my daughter using two utensils to steer the mouse, which at this time we thought was alone, from out of the basin for the barbeque.

My wife, who was a girl from the country, suggested that we should start up the barbeque with the mice in it. I on the other hand am much more humane then that, so I decided to get Nellie.

The problem came when Nellie was outside basking in the October fall sun. I called "here Nellie, Nellie" which was usually rewarded by food or cuddling up for a nap in bed.

Unfortunately when she was outside, it met being sent inside the house because everyone else was leaving.

I had to use some other coaxing to get close to her. "It's ok Nellie, you don't have to go inside, and I just want to put you inside the barbeque for a minute."

It is not quite known how much animals understand about the human language, but being told you are going to put inside anything, little own a barbeque, I am sure turns out to be very frightening.

She started to slink away. For those of you that do not understand the term "slink" because you do not have cats, I give the following explanation.

Let's say you were going into town for a minute for one drink with some old friends, and three hours later your wife walks into the Legion looking for you. This is where the art of slinking comes in handy, even more so if you can make yourself invisible.

The other arts useful at this time are lying and passing the blame to someone who has just left or "slinked out of the building". These you will find are all required tools to survive many years of married bliss.

As for Nellie, I finally had her corralled, and brought her over to the barbeque. Like in hunting season, it didn't take long to get the first chase underway. I showed Nellie the tail that was visible inside the barbeque and she became intent.

When the brown mouse eyes looked into the green cat eyes, the chase began. Out of the barbeque and across the patio table, then down under the wooden porch and the mouse chase was on.

My daughter let out a screech!

A second mouse was sitting on the edge of the barbeque, with its eyes bulged and whiskers twitching. I figured that it would be a good time for him to cut his losses and try and get away.

When Nellie was put on the payroll, she usually could catch her monies worth, and when she was done with his spouse, his twin, his co-worker, or whatever, this mouse was likely going be eaten.

So run my little mouse friend, run like the wind. Pretend you had never heard of Madoc, or paid first and last months rent for the barbeque.

Just run, so that you may pass on the legend of Nellie to your little mice offspring. In the memory of Tobo Gee Joe, just run!

Nellie had this other knack of trying to tick me off especially if she did not get fed when she wanted. It would usually involve going out into the yard and catching chipmunks and bringing them back for me to witness the execution.

This was something I could handle in moderation while walking by, but apparently this didn't do enough to satisfy her attention-seeking requirement.

She then decided it would be prudent to bring the animals inside the house to make sure that we had noticed what she had accomplished.

The first time you see a dead chipmunk on the kitchen floor while your daughter is preparing for her high school "Friends of the

Environment" class to come over, is a little overwhelming for everyone.

What is more interesting than that is the ability for a cat to be able to meow while it has something in its mouth. On this particular day Nellie came to the door and meowed to get in.

After letting her in, she headed underneath the kitchen table. I of course started a conversation with her in whom I asked if she had been chasing chipmunks, when low and behold one shot out form underneath the table.

Apparently if the dead chipmunks are not drawing enough attention from the owners of the house, than why in hell, not bring in a live one and let it go.

I looked at her and she looked at me, when I pointed out that for her sake she better do something about the chipmunk that was heading down the hallway towards the stairs. Especially before mother gets home!

For some reason they both took a detour into my office. Now if you realize how fond of mice I am, picture me with a chipmunk. A chipmunk is the "Hulk" of mice, and could hurt me bad enough to put me in the hospital.

So I went to the garage and got my hockey stick. Over the years as I slowed down I had found out that it had a lot more uses than just shooting the puck.

I opened the front door of the house and held it open with the hockey stick as I tried to get as far away from the pair of combatants. The chipmunk must have seen the light of day as he shot from the office with the cat in hot pursuit, with the only sound being that of nails trying to get traction on the hardwood floor.

The chipmunk made it away to live another day, the cat was ticked off until she found another one, and I learned to not open the door for the cat unless you could see what she had in her mouth!

Surviving the Marmora Jamboree

We have just returned home from a fun filled weekend of camping, visiting and of course, way too way much drinking. The music was excellent, the weather interesting and the people even better.

There is a lot of hard work by the Warren Family, their very close friends, and the many, many volunteers that make the weekend such a success. I commend them all on their hard work and commitment that make the weekend such an enjoyable event.

Now if you do not attend this specific event, I will let you substitute any event that ends in the words "Jamboree" to be able to follow this particular tale.

If you attend any Jamboree and you rough camp, two things are going to happen. One you are going to meet some very nice people over the course of the weekend and two, you are going to feel very "rough" before the weekend is out.

Now I suppose there are people that have enough common sense, or are now at the proper age, to be "grown up" as my mother used to say.

For some strange reason, at forty-four years old in the body of a sixty year old, I keep forgetting that ever so important speech.

There is just something about the cool September air, the grass beneath your feet and that cold, cold stare coming from your wife that makes the weekend memorable.

The part I can't figure out is why a person thinks that any time they are not sleeping, that they feel the need to consume alcohol.

It's like if you were home and had three days off, chances are you wouldn't reach for a beer when you first get to the fridge in the morning. Some milk, possibly some orange juice, damn it, even a pop would likely be better for you.

Not when you are rough camping. It's time to get back to my ancestral roots, drink like a man, hunt food as it passes by in the long grass, and look for the scent of the wild female as she passes by.

I don't really know a lot about the scent of the wild female thing back in the days of the caveman, but when rough camping, and you follow some hot filly, without makeup, to a seasoned "porta-potty", then drinking at seven in the morning does start to make a lot of sense!

Now don't get me wrong ladies, I am sure there are a lot of you that will lure the right male into following you. It will be usually based on age, soberness, and most of all, the amount of alimony payments already being paid to past adventures.

Then on the other hand, a lady heading to the washroom after sleeping all night, likely doesn't have "meeting some moron along the way", very high on her list. She likely just wants to get there, where there better be toilet paper and those little wipes you get from the chicken place.

The men don't really care about the little wipes; they just want the toilet paper, a bag full of leaves, or a really old shirt that they will finally give up and part with.

The use of wipes are frowned upon because your hands smell like you just got done eating at the chicken place and your wife has made you clean yourself up before driving "her" car anywhere like that.

My suggestion after having gone rough camping is to always pack some toilet paper.

The offering of an old shirt or leaves to a woman in the unit next to you, can usually lead to some very strange looks and possibly a visit from the "Security" people.

The first night was on a Thursday night, so if you are going to do things right, book off Friday, move in Thursday night and camp until Sunday.

Always camp with friends, definitely someone with First Aid, possibly someone with a Defibrillator and training (which I will get to later), and finally someone who maybe, just maybe, has an old ambulance with working lights.

I point out the training part because you have not seen scary until a campsite full of drunk people figure it would be a good time to wake someone up using the "battery charger machine, you know, the one with those little paddles, he, he, he".

I have been there and done that as they say, and I personally am looking forward to the day that the hair on my chest returns to normal and doesn't tingle when near anything electrical anymore.

Now that you have booked off Friday and have the rest of the weekend to relax, you should attempt to move in on Wednesday night and setup your campsite if possible. This works much better if you camp with people that have done it before and follow their instruction especially if you take anything bigger than a mini-van into your campsite.

Our first thought was my daughter's tent which fit in the back of our half ton pickup truck, but likely "too cold and too far for me to fall out of, when I have to go pee in the middle of the night".

Being a creative man and rebuilding my once classic fish hut design, I decided that we should take the "fish hut" to the Jamboree.

Before you judge my design too much, picture an eight foot by ten foot, steel metal shed which looks a lot like your normal utility shed in the city, but converts to "Stewie's fish hut" once hooked behind my four-wheeler and headed to the lake.

Of course I had to overcome the "I am not being seen in a fish hut with you at a Jamboree full of trailers and RV's". I suggested she kept the door shut until dark each night, which didn't help to win her over.

It looked like the tent in the back of the pick up was going to be the only option until the September nights were starting to get extremely cold. When I reminded her that the fish hut would have a wood stove she started to change her mind and then "she started to return to her ancestral roots".

It looked like there was a tie in the bi-election between the people when I would tell them what our plans were for accommodations for the Jamboree.

Some agreed that the fish hut was a good idea but most of them were fellow Legion members and between the drinking, the laughing, and the odd occasional, "He's taking a fish hut to the Jamboree" remarks, I thought everything would work out.

Then a very strange thing happened that changed our trip. I was looking out my bedroom window and looking across at the beautiful house that our neighbors, Ken and Theresa had built over three years ago, when I noticed it.

Their two boys were playing in front of this thing that was parked beside their house that resembled a camper trailer. I had seen it there before, had watched them leave with it on camping trips, and had seen them bring it home. Damn it, it was a camper trailer!

My wife sometimes tells me that my attention span isn't very good if I happen to be on another mission. As I asked my wife to repeat what she had said, I realized that Ken held the answer to my current dilemma. All I had to do was ask them to borrow the trailer.

Now most of you that know me will find this hard to believe, but I tend to be a bit pig headed, do it yourself, don't ask for help, kind of person.

In this case it was either staying in the back of the half ton in a tent, or finding a trailer big enough to take the "El Fish Hut".

It started with the "Ken old buddy" can I borrow your trailer?" and ended with Theresa and the boys both voting four to none for us to have the trailer.

I thought to myself how nice it is to have such good neighbors but found out later when talking with another neighbor, that Ken and Theresa decided to host a party for the neighborhood while we were away. They said it was the first good chance they had at peace since they moved in.

The trailer worked great for us and I heard the party was a great success. Even our two girls went while we were away.

Now with the trailer in tow, and some of the supplies packed, we headed to the Jamboree for the ever so important "setup". The setup is one of the most important processes of the Jamboree because if you try to do it when you have been drinking, all kind of bad things can happen.

First of all you have to get the trailer in the right spot, which is a lot easier to do in a field with only a few people in it, instead of a bunch.

On this night, the kind "Security" person finally said, "Why don't you drive it around in a circle instead of backing up?" followed a few minutes later by, "Well you know where your site is, good luck getting the trailer in it."

Rule number two is to park your trailer so that you can pull it straight out if and when you need to go home. Trying to navigate through a maze on Sunday would have killed me, with or without the defibrillator.

While parking your trailer on your site, I have found there are two important steps to consider. One is level ground and the other is blocking of the wheels. Both very important first steps, although remembering how funny it was to see my wife's eyes looking out the trailer door, as it rolled down the hill after unhooking it from my truck, was priceless.

I haven't seen anything that classic since watching the Flintstones as a child.

The leveling part is also very important, mainly because you do not want to wake up in the middle of the night having to go to the bathroom, and have to fight your way uphill to do it. It is a lot easier to navigate on flat ground, than it is on an incline.

Sleeping also works a lot better when the trailer is somewhat flat. Rolling out of bed in the middle of the night is usually not high on anyone's list, and if you get lucky enough for a piece of tail, you definitely don't want that to roll out of site half way through.

Once you have the site set up and the trailer leveled and blocked, you can get on to the more important things. Such as drinking, drinking, and more drinking.

Of course, if you would like to enjoy the whole weekend, it might be best to set out some type of agenda for the weekend.

Start with Thursday night. Your objective could be to have some drinks, meet the people next to you, and try to locate landmarks that will help you recognize where your campsite is.

Try to avoid using landmarks such as "the big lady in the white sweater", or odds are you will end up sleeping under a table at the Fireman's Bingo on Saturday morning. Also don't choose things like the green colored outhouse. There are way too many of them to get lost by.

Try to use things like, "I wish I had enough money to buy something like this", or "this sure looks a lot bigger than my fish hut".

These types of landmarks will help you, and better yet, the people that are trying to get you off their campsite and back on the way to yours will be overly hospitable.

So it is very, very important to listen to them the first time to avoid being sent the wrong way the next night.

Try to think of it as living in different parts of a city. You have the high income, beautiful corporate homes, and the middle class smaller working couple homes, and finally us, the people with the trailer that looks a lot like a fish hut. But don't let that bother you, because we will end up drinking a lot more, and having a lot more fun than those people that actually look after themselves.

Chances are we will likely be getting a kidney from them sometime after their baby boomer stock portfolio crashes, and they end up jumping out their office window.

That's what is nice about having different classes of people, who are willing to share organs after their death.

Most of the people I knew wanted to share their organ with someone. More precisely, let's make that anyone, before his or her death.

Although the organ they wanted to share, wasn't what anyone really wanted, but unfortunately it did more thinking for them than any other part of their body when they were drinking. That was mainly because they didn't have a plan laid out for the whole weekend at the jamboree.

Once you have located your campsite, make sure you leave identifying marks around "your" trailer. If you have come this far on your own, there is no need to screw up the weekend by wandering into someone else's camper on your site.

People like to camp with you in their group, but when it comes time to sleep, they tend to like to do it on their own. It is not usually negotiable, and if it is, you my dear friend are going to pay later down the road.

Mother-in-law playing, "Box Car Willie's Mule Train a Coming" at six in the morning type of payback. That is not pretty with a two-day hangover and four hours sleep.

Another important aspect that I forgot but my wife remembered, is to have your bed already made up before you head out on your first night of socializing. Because when you get back to the trailer, it sure does make life a lot easier.

The only problem had been that she had traded our queen size bed from home into a doublewide cot, and for some strange reason, she felt it belonged to her. I don't know if it was because she made the bed, or if she knew it was going to be cold that night and she huddled in as if it was a rugby scrum.

Either way, I was not going to win, so with a beer near the head of my bed, I knew I would have to improvise.

That usually consists of lying still in one spot until you hear her start to snore, and then slowly try to work yourself under a third of the covers. It is very important to not try and take too many covers at once, because remember the story about waking the sleeping giant. That site isn't very pretty. Let them sleep, and try to get her to go to Bingo in the morning, long enough for you to get caught up on some sleep.

We awoke on Friday morning with the giant in a good mood after her good nights sleep. I myself was in one of those moods where I couldn't really tell if I was hung over yet, or just tired from getting done a weeks work.

I would have to wait to later in the day before I would base my decision, on which was which.

The giant decided to make us some lunch after while before having to leave for town on a scheduled restocking mission. I looked in my cooler and realized that the two bags of ice I had purchased had changed to water.

If there had of been Sunday gospel singing going on, I possibly could have taken it to the stage and tried to get it changed into wine, which really wouldn't help me.

I decided that without ice, chances were that my beer was going to get warm. So I thought it best that maybe, just maybe, we could drink maybe one or two, until we made a run to town.

It was a very bad idea drinking the first one and a not so bad idea for the second one. I really didn't see any problem with the third one.

Well we progressed into town long enough to restock the beer and the ice and then returned to the jamboree. My wife had to head out to a scheduled event, which left me all alone to go and meet the neighbors.

The one thing I learned early in life was if you were going to go on a mission, make sure you pack supplies. I was packing when my wife informed me that she didn't have to leave right away and that she was coming with me to scout out the other campsites. We searched high and low for people we knew were supposed to be there, but eventually came to the conclusion that most of them were not coming in until Friday night.

Although, I was a little suspicious of the great number of people running into their trailers and pulling their blinds as we walked up towards them.

We headed back to our campsite and had a visit with our fellow campers, which actually consisted of me talking, my wife getting ready to leave, and the other couple trying to relax and read a book.

After my wife left, an overwhelming thought came over me that I had seen a friend of mine drive by with a Home Hardware golf cart. He was busy working the Fireman's Bingo, but I had to go and try to get him to help me find my lost friends at the jamboree.

Sure enough, after he was done we headed around the campground looking for the people that were lost. Eventually his girlfriend tracked him down and said that he was in charge of feeding the volunteer fireman and to get off the cart, so I thought my mission was doomed.

I then asked to use the cart, and Scott agreed as he told me to be careful. So my next half hour was touring the campgrounds, where I eventually found some friends right behind the sign listing my name as one of the people that were not allowed in that section. It was in pen on a ripped piece of cardboard and was starting to fade. I thought it should be all right then.

The other funny thing was I started to deliver older people who were walking to their campsite, after they asked for a ride. I would ask them if they liked Home Hardware and the answer always came up yes.

I even stopped at a couple of sights and asked if they had ordered the four by eight sheets of plywood, which brought a few chuckles. I found that the people at Jamborees are usually pretty fun!

I took back the cart, thanked Scott and Mary Anne and headed back to restock before going to visit. I ended up at a site consisting of my neighbors up the road, where I had quite a nice visit and just tried to stay out of the sun.

It wasn't long after that, the music started to play. It was late afternoon and the crowd was starting to build.

Thursday night was a good show with a decent crowd, but by Friday night you could feel the atmosphere starting to build.

With chairs in hand, and the cooler packed, we headed to the stage. The headliner was Tommy Cash, brother of Johnny Cash, and as the crowd grew, so did the enthusiasm.

All of the acts leading up to the show just set the stage for a great show, and when the headliner hit the stage, the show was in full gear.

It was a very entertaining and enjoyable show, with a special spot in it where Tommy invited a young girl to sing with him. She had sung earlier in the show before he had come out, but when she came back out, they did the song "Jackson", with Tommy singing the part of his brother John, and this young lady singing the part of his wife.

She didn't miss a beat, and her actions on stage were priceless, as she was a true performer. Her name eludes me now, but I am sure it will show up in years to come.

It was at this point and time in the night that I realized what all the hard work was for. In the small town of Marmora, Ontario, Canada, we were watching legends who came to sing, and new ones starting out.

After the Friday night show, most of my counterparts including my wife, decided to go visiting with the help of Mike and Mandy, two crazy people that wandered onto our campsite.

Unlike Mork and Mindy, the loveable television alien and his roommate from the early seventies, these pair hadn't likely even been born yet.

They were still full of piss and vinegar and convinced three quarters of our group that they were all young enough to survive. It was too late in the day for me, and tonight the doublewide cot had my name on it.

The next thing I heard was them leaving in the wee hours of the morning because Mike had to be somewhere to hunt geese by daybreak, and finally then it was a chance to get back to sleep.

Saturday turned out to be bright and sunny with a nice gentle breeze as the day started. What no one realized is that someone must have ticked off the man upstairs, because he decided to turn the fan from the "low" setting to the "really, really high" setting by mid afternoon. The winds picked up to mid hurricane status and then the fun began.

The jamboree is set along side the Marmora Mine, which is an open pit mine over a mile deep. On the outside of the mine are big, enormous piles of slag from the waste in the mine, which can be seen for miles and miles around. It makes a picturesque setting for the backdrop of all the trailers and fish huts at the jamboree.

On this specific day we set a record. It turned out in Marmora's history it was the first time that three different people tried to Para-sail over the mine in one day. It turns out they were just people trying to hold down their tents when the storm blew in.

The other record was for the largest yard sale ever held on Sunday at the Jamboree. The people along the west fence line hosted the yard sale. It turned out that they had all kinds of stuff they didn't come with after the storm hit than what they did before.

Lastly, I was able to make some extra cash myself. Once the first portable outhouse blew over in the storm, the owner paid me to use my two hundred and fifty pounds, to sit in one of his until the storm blew past. I told my wife that this extra weight would come in handy some time. I just wish I had of had my laptop to keep me busy while I was in there.

Once the storm subsided and everyone got their bearings back, we returned back to the camp sit for a beautiful potluck dinner as a group. After that was done it was time to restock and head back to the stage for another great night of music.

By the second night I was like a dog tearing at his leash. There is something about the bright lights, a great crowd and great entertainment. I had to find a way on stage, but the exact quote from my wife was, "If he goes on stage, I am going home".

I did make it backstage to meet Tommy Cash on Friday and George Fox on Saturday. Maybe next year some MC work might fit me in without my wife knowing, with of course a little comedy. I will let her know in advance, so this time when the "Security" people bring me back, they know we are working together.

Again all the acts leading up to George Fox were top notch and his headlining performance was spectacular. It was quite moving to see where he started out and where he is today. He is a truly talented performer that remembers his roots and his dreams, and is an inspiration to us all in the entertainment business.

Saturday night wound down with the "open mike" portion of the show, as did Thursday nights show. It involved some talented professional's right down to someone fulfilling their dream to be on stage in front of a big crowd for the very first time.

Saturday night was my night to go visiting, which seemed like a good idea at the time, but seeing I was on my own, the others must have learned their lesson the night before. I didn't vote highly for the choice I had made the night before, when it became Sunday morning.

Sunday morning came with the sound of light rain on the outside of my head and the sound of a pending thunderstorm inside my head. I decide that it would be prudent to pull up stakes as early as possible.

The amazing thing was the trailer went on the hitch of my truck on the very first try, which is usually a definite sign that it will drop off the truck on the way home.

With my wife loading the truck, me putting away the blocking for the trailer, I was glad I had remembered rule number one.

Always park so that it is easier to get out when you go to leave. Finally, we were ready, and with a goodbye and thank you to our friends for letting us camp with them, we headed on our trip home.

As we left the field, I noticed a group of six people having coffee and visiting at a trailer.

I spoke to them and said, "We have to go home now, and my wife is all jamboreed out." The group laughed and some kind woman pointed out that I had a window still open on the camper and wondered if that was ok to travel that way.

I replied, "It's ok, she is still sleeping and I haven't told her we were leaving yet!" That final thought and interaction with others is what made the whole weekend worthwhile.

We live in a good world when strangers are making friends with one common goal, "Happiness, kindness, and a love of Country Music".

Some Final Thoughts

In my life I have done some strange things in the quest to make people laugh, or to make them just feel good about themselves. I have always believed that we are only here once and that we only have one chance in life to try and get things somewhat right.

Therefore I will leave you with a few stories about myself but will end on a note telling a tale of a remarkable man who had the extraordinary ability to make people of all ages laugh. His keen sense of humor, his timing and the manner in which he carried on, left us all with great memories of laughter and joy, no matter what age you were.

He was a friend that I always looked forward to visiting with and today I get to share some of his stories with you.

But first we must tie up a few loose ends. I was the possibly the only person on record to request four beer to go at a hockey tournament.

When questioned by the people running the tournament on how I was going to get them out of the arena without anyone seeing me, I replied that I was going to use the baby seat. So with my wife carrying the baby, and me carrying the baby seat full of beer all covered in blankets, we headed out of the arena on our way home.

The only problem came when I asked my wife if she had put my equipment in the van before we left the arena. Apparently she hadn't, so I had to make a call back and have someone bring it up to me the next time they were up our way.

When my wife asked how I could forget it, I replied that I was carrying the baby.

Another time I was asked by friends of mine to wear a gorilla suit at a man's retirement party from GM. When I picked the suit up in the afternoon, I brought it home after a few drinks with some friends.

For some strange reason again, I thought that it would be a good idea to get into character and practice being an ape by scaring my wife and daughters who were out for a walk. So I donned the suit and waited patiently around the corner of the house, as I watched them coming up the lane way.

As they got close enough, I jumped out from behind the building and let out a roar. They all jumped and let out screams which was soon followed by laughter. All except for the fact that I forgot our dog was with them. Instead of laughter, there was this intense growling sound coming from her, with the hair standing up on her back.

Knowing that I had to do something quick or end up being bit, I quickly peeled the head of the suit off. The look on the dog's face changed to one of happiness now that she could see who it was. Until she looked down at the hair on my body and wondered what this ape was doing with my head. The growling started again.

I had my wife and kids hold her down until I could get inside the house and get out of the suit. I sometimes wonder why I let myself get into these things, which always seem to be a good idea at the time.

Now it is time to hear a few tales of my good friend Wilfred. If you grew up in Marmora and didn't get the chance to meet this man and listen to any of his tales, you truly did miss out on his ability to story tell. I just hope I do him justice as I recount some of his tales.

Back before 911 and pagers, the Marmora Fire Department like all others used a special phone system in each home of the firefighters plus the use of a siren at the fire hall. This siren had a unique sound to it that could be heard for miles away, and when it sounded the firemen from the village would race to the fire hall.

The only other unique sound, which was identical to the fire siren, just happened to come from Wilfred. He had this ability to recreate the sound of the siren so well; that he could constantly fool the firemen into thinking the real one had gone off. He would of course use this to his advantage on Friday afternoons.

If I have the story right, when the Marmora Mine was going strong, a person had to be at the Marmora Hotel by noon to get a seat on a Friday afternoon. If you were late, then there was no way to get a seat near the bar or at a table.

That was of course if you could make a sound like the fire siren. On this day Wilfred was late and noticed the Fire Chief's van parked outside the hotel. When he looked inside he saw him sitting at the bar, so he went back outside and let loose with his rendition of the fire siren.

As the Chief came outside and headed to the fire hall, Wilfred went in. He not only took his seat, but also was drinking his beer when the Fire Chief got back.

Wilfred also looked after his son and brother's garage when they were away. On this particular day a woman pulled in during the pouring rain.

As Wilfred went up to the car, she rolled down the window a crack and said to put five dollars worth of gas in the vehicle. She also asked that he check the oil. After doing so he informed her that it needed a quart.

She told him that there was one in the trunk, which he retrieved and put in the vehicle.

When he went to collect the five dollars, he sarcastically asked, "Do you take your own buns to McDonalds?"

Wilfred also worked with a young man named Radar who was built low to the ground. One day Radar had found an old basketball, which was half deflated, and while putting in time, he was playing with it trying to bounce the ball. Wilfred had a customer at the time and said that Radar was his son, and that the Toronto Raptors had just drafted him. He said that he wasn't that tall but he was really fast.

The customer just shook his head and got back in his car.

My final thought comes from something that just happened the other day while we were in Oshawa at Durham College watching my daughter's team play Fastball.

I was walking along past a couple that had two dogs on leashes. One was a Dalmatian and the other a mixed breed. I joked with the one owner that there were some men on a fire truck looking for his dog while petting the Dalmatian. After I was done I reached over and petted the second dog, when the owner spoke up and said that she was surprised the dog let me do that.

I don't know about you, but to me that might sound a lot like, "I can't believe she didn't bite you." Something they maybe should have told me before I started to reach for her.

Anyhow it reminded me of the old story of the man sitting in the park with a dog sitting beside him. When a stranger came along he asked if his dog bites and the man replied "No". As he reaches for the dog, it latches onto his hand and bites him.

When the man questions the man on the bench about what he had told him about his dog, he replied, "It's not my dog!"

I guess that it just goes to show that sometimes a lot can be said about a person by how little they say.

To all those great storytellers that I have been privileged to call friends, I hope that I have told your tales so that they can live on for future generations to share and cherish.

It will be their job to put their own twist to each tale and to recount their own memory as how it was told to them. With that the tale will never get old, but only better and better throughout the years to come.

So until we have the chance to talk again, make sure you listen to that little child's story the next time you hear it. In the end, it might not all be make believe.